Walk Around

P-38 Lightning

By Larry Davis

Color by Don Greer

Illustrated by Dave Gebhardt and Darren Glenn

Walk Around Number 30

squadron/signal publications

Introduction

The pilots of Hitler's Luftwaffe called the Lockheed **P-38 Lightning** *der Gabelschwanz Teufel* – the 'Forked-Tail Devil' – after facing it over North Africa. The P-38 was the most advanced aircraft of its time. Its pilot sat in a nacelle slung between two engine booms, each housing one Allison V-1710 engine. This power enabled the Lightning to exceed 400 MPH (643.7 KMH). The nacelle also housed the armament of four .50 caliber (12.7MM) machine guns and a large bore cannon.

The Lightning began with the **XP-38** prototype of 1939; the basic design was little changed between the **YP-38** of 1940 and the **P-38H** of 1942. The two V-1710 engines were fitted into streamlined nacelles, with General Electric turbo-superchargers mounted atop the mid-nacelle. A vertical tail assembly was mounted onto each nacelle, while a single horizontal stabilizer connected the tail assemblies. This unique configuration resulted in the German nickname of 'Forked-Tail Devil.' The P-38 was also the world's first production aircraft equipped with a tricycle landing gear.

The **P-38-LO** was the first production Lightning variant, which equipped the 1st Pursuit Group (Fighter Group from 1942), US Army Air Corps (later Army Air Forces) in mid-1941. The **P-38D**, **P-38E**, **P-38F**, **P-38G**, and P-38H soon followed off Lockheed's production line. These variants had little external changes, with the major differences between them being upgraded engines and instruments.

A 20MM weapon on the P-38E and later models replaced the 37MM cannon that armed early Lightnings. The upper canopy was changed from a starboard side-opening model to an aft hinged item on late production P-38Fs. Early Lightning variants saw action with USAAF squadrons in theaters ranging from Alaska and North Africa to the South Pacific.

In November of 1942, the **P-38J** introduced significant changes in the Lightning's external appearance. Lockheed moved the supercharger intercoolers from the wing leading edge to an open front intake directly under the propeller spinner. This resulted in the distinct 'chin' that identified late model P-38s. The P-38J was powered by two 1425 HP V-1710-F17 engines, which gave it a maximum speed of 414 MPH (666.3 KMH), while it had a range of 1400 miles (2253 KM). Only the North American P-51 Mustang exceeded the Lightning's speed and range. Lockheed built 9923 Lightnings, ending with the **P-38M Night Lightning** night fighter in 1945.

The Lightning airframe also found major success in the **F-4/F-5** photo-reconnaissance aircraft series. The **F-4** and **F-4A** used the P-38 airframe, while the **F-5A** was derived from the P-38G. Later reconnaissance Lightnings – the **F-5B**, **F-5C**, **F-5E**, **F-5F**, and **F-5G** – used the P-38J/L airframe. Lockheed replaced the armament with various camera suites in all F-4s and F-5s. These cameras usually included at least two oblique cameras in the center nacelle sides and a vertical camera on the nose undersurface. F-4s and F-5s were the primary USAAF tactical reconnaissance aircraft in all major theaters of World War Two, although the F-6 Mustang was a close second. Additionally, the air forces of Free France, China, and Australia flew reconnaissance Lightnings during the conflict.

After the war ended in 1945, the USAAF rapidly phased out the P-38/F-4/F-5 in favor of jet aircraft. Lightnings remained in service with France (F-5G), Nationalist China (F-5E), Honduras (P-38J), and other countries into the 1950s. Many civilian contractors also flew Lightnings as weather aircraft, air racers, and high-speed passenger aircraft in the post-war period.

This book primarily covers the P-38J day fighter; however, there is also detailed coverage of the F-4/F-5 reconnaissance aircraft and the P-38M Night Lightning. The author wishes to thank Mr. Keith Melville for his detailed photos of the P-38J restored at Duxford, England, and Ms. Nicole Vannatter at the US Air Force Museum (USAFM) for help in photographing the P-38J displayed there. Sadly, Duxford's Lightning was destroyed in a flying accident in the fall of 1996. Lastly, thanks to Mr. Eric Schulzinger at Lockheed Historical Archives in the old Burbank, California plant – the original production facility for the P-38 series – for supplying many detailed photos of the 'Forked-Tail Devil.'

ISBN 0-89747-453-8

If you have any photographs of aircraft, armor, soldiers or ships of any nation, particularly wartime snapshots, why not share them with us and help make Squadron/Signal's books all the more interesting and complete in the future. Any photograph sent to us will be copied and the original returned. The donor will be fully credited for any photos used. Please send them to:

Squadron/Signal Publications, Inc.
1115 Crowley Drive
Carrollton, TX 75011-5010

Если у вас есть фотографии самолётов, вооружения, солдат или кораблей любой страны, особенно, снимки времён войны, поделитесь с нами и помогите сделать новые книги издательства Эскадрон/Сигнал ещё интереснее. Мы переснимем ваши фотографии и вернём оригиналы. Имена приславших снимки будут сопровождать все опубликованные фотографии. Пожалуйста, присылайте фотографии по адресу:

Squadron/Signal Publications, Inc.
1115 Crowley Drive
Carrollton, TX 75011-5010

軍用機、装甲車両、兵士、軍艦などの写真を所持しておられる方は いらっしゃいませんか？どの国のものでも結構です。作戦中に撮影されたものが特に良いのです。Squadron/Signal社の出版する刊行物において、このような写真は内容を一層充実し、興味深くすることができます。当方にお送り頂いた写真は、複写の後お返しいたします。出版物中に写真を使用した場合は、必ず提供者のお名前を明記させて頂きます。お写真は下記にご送付ください。

Squadron/Signal Publications, Inc.
1115 Crowley Drive
Carrollton, TX 75011-5010

(Front Cover) Col Charles H. MacDonald taxis his fourth PUTT PUTT MARU, a P-38L (100/44-25643), in early 1945. MacDonald commanded the 475th Fighter Group (FG) at Clark Field, Luzon, the Philippines. His 27 victories were fifth highest among USAAF pilots during World War Two.

(Previous Page) Lockheed test pilot Marshall Headle flies the first YP-38 (2202/39-689) over southern California in late 1940. This service test variant led to all subsequent P-38/F-4/F-5 Lightning models. (Lockheed)

(Rear Cover) The F-5E *Kate* (S9/42-8624) flies over northern France on 6 June 1944. This aircraft was assigned to the 34th Photographic Reconnaissance Squadron (PRS), 10th Photographic Group at Chalgrove, England. Black and white 'Invasion Stripes' marked aircraft assigned to the Allied invasion of Normandy.

The sole XP-38 (37-457) was rolled out of Lockheed's Burbank, California plant on 27 January 1939. The sharply pointed engine nacelle shape was changed to a broader nacelle on the YP-38 prototype and subsequent production aircraft. This fighter was equipped with General Electric (GE) type F turbo-superchargers, which were mounted atop the tail booms. Supercharger air intakes were mounted immediately aft and above the wing leading edge, while carburetor intakes were located under the wing trailing edge. The XP-38 was left in natural metal, while the rudders were painted with a glossy Insignia Blue (FS15044) vertical stripe and seven glossy Insignia Red (FS11136) and six glossy Insignia White (FS17875) horizontal stripes. (Lockheed)

The butterfly yoke atop the control column is mounted in the XP-38 cockpit mockup. Lockheed engineers used this mockup to confirm the placement of instruments and controls. The control column was angled from the starboard side, while the engine throttles were located to port. Cardboard facsimiles were used for many of the instruments in this mockup. (Lockheed)

The XP-38's two 1150 HP Allison V-1710C-9 engines turned three-bladed Hamilton Standard propellers, which rotated opposite of each other to counter engine torque effects. Initial test flights revealed a maximum speed of 420 MPH (675.9 KMH). The XP-38 was lost while attempting to land at Mitchel Field, New York on 11 February 1939. A Douglas B-18 Bolo bomber is parked in the background. (Lockheed)

(Above) One of the 13 YP-38s is parked on the Lockheed ramp in late 1940. This service test model differed from the XP-38 prototype in several ways. These included the newly designed engine oil coolers, which were faired into the underside of the forward engine nacelles. The coolant radiators on the aft portion of the engine nacelles were also enlarged on the YP-38. This variant introduced three-bladed Curtiss Electric propellers that turned outboard to improve airflow over the tail. Turning the propellers were two 1150 HP Allison V-1710F engines. (Lockheed)

(Left) A YP-38 equipped with four 'dummy' .50 caliber (12.7MM) nose mounted machine guns makes a test flight out from Burbank in 1940. Streamlined fairings on the nose tested the aerodynamic effects of these weapons on the aircraft. The oil cooler openings under the propellers were enlarged over those fitted to the earlier XP-38. Small carburetor air intake scoops were mounted on the outboard nacelle sides aft of the wing trailing edges. US military aircraft had the national insignia painted only on the wings before October of 1940. U.S. ARMY painted under the wings is Glossy Black, later called Jet Black (FS17038). (USAF)

(Above) One of the Model 322 Lightning Mk Is for Britain's Royal Air Force (RAF) flies off the California coast during the late summer of 1941. The fighter's upper surfaces are painted in the RAF camouflage colors of Dark Green (FS34079) and Dark Earth (FS30118), with Sky (FS34504) undersurfaces. The US government would not allow the export of engine superchargers at the time; thus, the Lightning Is were powered by non-supercharged 1090 HP Allison V-1710-C15 engines turning both propellers to starboard. The RAF ordered 143 Lightning Is, but only accepted three aircraft and none of these saw combat. (Lockheed)

(Right) A P-322-II Lightning II (AF207) warms up its engines prior to a mission from Hamilton Field, California in 1942. This fighter was one of 140 aircraft from the cancelled RAF order taken over by the US Army Air Forces (USAAF). The Lightning IIs followed 23 P-322 Lightning Is commandeered by the US in early 1942. The P-322-II's Allison V-1710-F2 engines turned their propellers to starboard. These Lightnings had US markings painted on the RAF camouflage scheme. P-322s were flown on training and air defense missions in the Continental US. (USAF)

Several YP-38s are lined up in the final assembly area of Lockheed's Burbank plant in the spring of 1941. The near aircraft lacks the outer wing section and access panels for the starboard V-1710 engine, which is being run up. Pointed propeller spinners were changed to blunter models beginning with the P-38-LO. The turbo-supercharger cooling scoop is mounted atop the wing. Two Lockheed Hudsons for the RAF are parked to the rear. (Lockheed)

A Lightning pilot closes the side-opening canopy of this early P-38. This type of cockpit enclosure was used on all P-38-LO through P-38E aircraft and some P-38Fs and P-38Gs. A rear-opening canopy replaced the side-opening enclosure beginning with the P-38H. Both side windows were rolled up and down like those on an automobile. Bulletproof glass inside the windshield was introduced on the P-38-LO. (Lockheed via John Clements)

Four pilots huddle for a pre-flight briefing in front of a P-38-LO, while maintenance crews prepare this and two other Lightnings for flight. The P-38-LO was the first production variant and incorporated several changes from the prototype and service test models. The armament was standardized on four .50 caliber Browning M2 machine guns and one 37MM Browning M9 cannon in the nose. Lockheed built only 29 P-38-LOs in early 1941. (Lockheed)

A P-322 Lightning I (3006/AE983) is parked on a US airfield in early 1942. Most P-322s were pressed into USAAF service defending the US West Coast following the Pearl Harbor attack of 7 December 1941. Still designated P-322 rather than P-38, the Lightning Is retained both their RAF camouflage and serial number, but with early US 'red-center' insignia and U.S. ARMY under the wings. (Via Keith Melville)

This P-38-LO (56 1P) was assigned to the 1st Pursuit Group (PG) at Selfridge Field, Michigan in the summer of 1941. Essentially the same aircraft as the YP-38, the P-38-LO had the supercharger intake scoop atop the engine nacelle and the new blunt nose propeller spinners. The dual 'guns' in the nose are mockups. The Lightning is painted Olive Drab (FS34087) over Neutral Gray (FS36173). (Art Krieger)

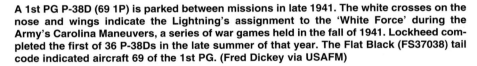

A 1st PG P-38D (69 1P) is parked between missions in late 1941. The white crosses on the nose and wings indicate the Lightning's assignment to the 'White Force' during the Army's Carolina Maneuvers, a series of war games held in the fall of 1941. Lockheed completed the first of 36 P-38Ds in the late summer of that year. The Flat Black (FS37038) tail code indicated aircraft 69 of the 1st PG. (Fred Dickey via USAFM)

Another 'White Force' P-38D of the 1st PG is parked at Goodfellow Field, Texas in the early fall of 1941. It had taken part in the Louisiana Maneuvers the previous August. This Lightning is fitted with the pointed spinners normally associated with YP-38s. Water-based white paint was used for the cross on the nose, which allowed ground crews to remove the markings after the exercise. (W.L. Bannister)

7

A 1st PG pilot climbs into SNUFFY, his P-38-LO in the fall of 1941. This aircraft is painted with the 'Red Force' cross during the Carolina Maneuvers. The P-38-LO was the first Lightning variant finished in the Olive Drab over Neutral Gray camouflage scheme. The propeller blade fronts are left in natural metal, while the backs were Flat Black to reduce glare for the pilot. The wheels, landing gear, gear door inner surfaces, and gear bays were left in natural metal at the time. Two simulated .50 caliber machine gun barrels are mounted on the nose. (USAF)

The pilot of this P-322-II (AF116) warms up his engines on the ramp at Hamilton Field in 1942. After the RAF accepted three P-322 Lightning Is in early 1942, the USAAF used the remaining 140 aircraft built to defend the West Coast against the Japanese threat. The US insignia – whose center red disc was deleted from 1 June 1942 – was painted over the British roundels on the fuselage and wings. Oil cooler inlets were more circular and set further aft on the P-322 compared to the earlier YP-38 and P-38-LO. This variant was armed with two .50 caliber and two .30 caliber (7.62MM) machine guns, while the 37MM cannon was deleted. In 1943, P-322s were reassigned from defending the US West Coast to training future P-38 pilots. (USAF)

A P-38F assigned to the 55th Fighter Group (FG) is parked on the ramp at Nuthampstead, England in late 1943. This Group was the second P-38 unit assigned to the 8th Air Force in October of 1943, but was the first to retain Lightnings for substantial combat operations. All wheels are fitted with hub caps, which were standard on early P-38s operating from the mud and grass of English airfields. The USAAF renamed its Pursuit units as Fighter units on 15 May 1942. (USAFM)

A factory fresh P-38H (42-67079) flies over Southern California during an acceptance flight in mid-1943. On 26 June 1943, the US national insignia was changed to include an Insignia Red outline and Insignia White side bars. The red border was replaced by one of Insignia Blue from 31 July 1943. Extreme heat of the turbo-supercharger burned the Olive Drab paint off the surrounding area and Lockheed stopped painting the areas on later production Lightnings. The tail number (267079) is painted Flat Orange Yellow (FS33538). (Lockheed)

9

The cockpit of this P-38G-15 (43-2337) was typical for early Lightnings (P-38-LOs through P-38Hs). The control column had a wheel for operating the ailerons, while moving the column fore and aft operated the elevators. Weapons were fired using a button mounted on the control wheel's starboard side. Throttles and propeller pitch controls were located on the port side console. An armored glass panel was mounted inside the windshield. (USAFM)

The central cockpit console held the fuel primer and oxygen regulator. Rudder pedals were placed immediately above the cockpit floor. Radio controls were mounted along the starboard cockpit wall, along with circuit breakers and the flap control panel. The pilot's seat incorporated a recess to accommodate a parachute, which also served as a seat cushion. P-38 cockpit interiors were painted ANA 611 Interior Green (FS34151), with instrument panels and consoles in semigloss Instrument Black (FS27038). (USAFM)

The P-38G's main instrument panel was quite similar to panels on other early P-38s. The type N-9 gun sight was mounted atop the panel, with a ring-and-bead backup sight immediately to port. The defroster tube fitted under the windshield fed hot air from the engines onto the windshield interior to keep this clear. (The armored glass panel was removed for this photo). The main electrical switch box was located just below and in front of the instrument panel. The large gun-charging handle was fitted to the port end of the main switch panel. Engine instruments were mounted on the instrument panel's port side, while flight instruments were located in the center and to starboard. The control column arm runs from the cockpit floor along the starboard wall, with the control wheel (unseen here) directly to the pilot's front. Cockpit instruments are reflected in the curved Plexiglas quarterlight panels. (Lockheed)

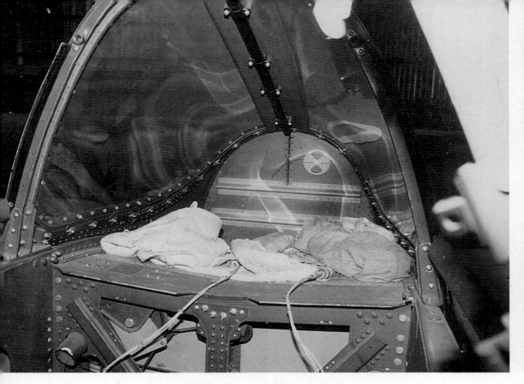

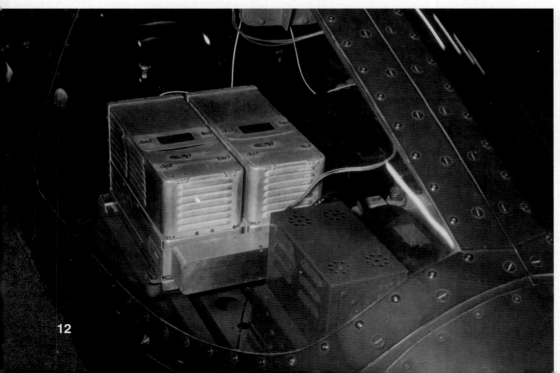

(Above Left) The P-38E's aft canopy extended toward a bulkhead inside the canopy surface. The all-around canopy gave Lightning pilots good overall visibility in air combat. The aft canopy section has a central frame running from the canopy arch to the aft bulkhead. Internal framing was painted Interior Green to match the cockpit areas. Some portions of this fighter's aft cockpit section are Chromate Yellow Primer (FS33481). Aircraft restorers left some towels in the aft cockpit area. (Via John Clements)

(Above) The cockpit seat is removed to reveal the P-38's lower aft floor and bulkhead. Reinforcement framing is placed along the cockpit aft bulkhead for additional strength. Some of the control cables run along the cockpit floor. These cables connected the rudder pedals to the rudders and the control column to the elevator and ailerons. (John Clements)

(Left) Radio equipment is installed on a rack mounted immediately aft of the pilot's seat. P-38s used a variety of radio equipment throughout its service history. Among the radios fitted to Lightning variants were the SCR-522, SCR-274N, and the SCR-695-A. The black radio box was mounted on the starboard side, while its generator was placed alongside in the aluminum box. The dive recovery flap control motor is mounted at the aft end of the equipment rack, immediately forward of aft canopy bulkhead. (Author)

(Above) The antenna relay box was mounted on the aft canopy's main support frame. Copper wires from the radio sets and generator were plugged into this box, which connected with the antenna cables. These cables ran from the aft canopy to the leading edges of both vertical stabilizers. A non-standard seat cushion is fitted to this restored P-38. This aircraft lacks the rear seat armor plating normally found on production Lightnings. (Author)

(Above Right) A radio transmission and receiving set is placed on the starboard section of the radio rack, immediately aft of the pilot's seat. The electrical generator alongside the radio supplied power for the radio and for the P-38's other electrical systems, which included the cockpit and navigation lights and the propeller pitch controls. The dive recovery flap control motor is located on the aft port section of this deck, immediately forward of the bulkhead. This motor sent power to the dive recovery flap drive motors located in the wings. These flaps were added to the lower wing surfaces on P-38J-25-LOs and retrofitted to earlier Lightnings in service. (Author)

(Right) A single wire connects both electrical generator boxes to the antenna relay box. Another wire leads from the radio set to the relay box. Both radios and generators for P-38s improved in performance during World War Two and updated equipment was mounted into Lightnings during its production life. (Author)

XP-38

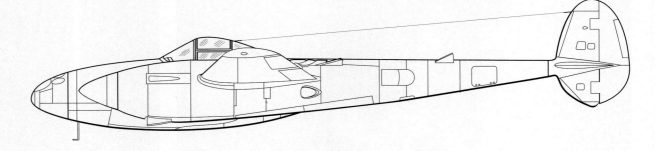

P-322 (Lightning Mk I)

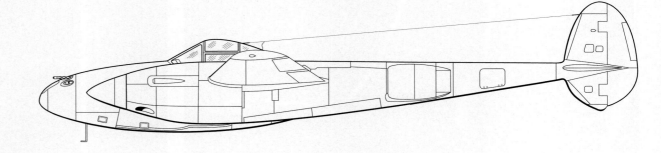

F-4A

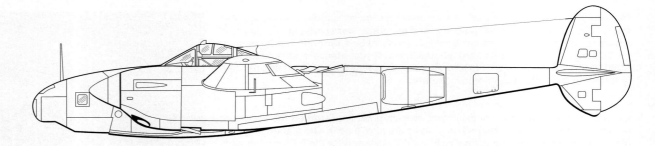

Lockheed P-38F Lightning Specifications

Wingspan:...............52 feet (15.8 M)
Length:....................37 feet 10 inches (11.5 M)
Height:....................12 feet 10 inches (3.9 M)
Empty Weight:........13,000 pounds (5896.8 KG)
Maximum Weight:..15,800 pounds (7166.9 KG)
Powerplant:.............Two 1225 HP Allison V-1710-49/53 12-cylinder,
                        liquid-cooled, inline engines

Armament:...............One 20MM Bendix M1 cannon with 150 rounds and
                        four .50 caliber (12.7MM) Browning M2 machine
                        guns with 500 rounds per gun in the nose.
Performance:
  Maximum Speed:..395 MPH (635.7 KMH) at 25,000 feet (7620 M)
  Service Ceiling:....39,000 feet (11,887.2 M)
  Range:...................1750 miles (2816.3 KM)
Crew:......................One

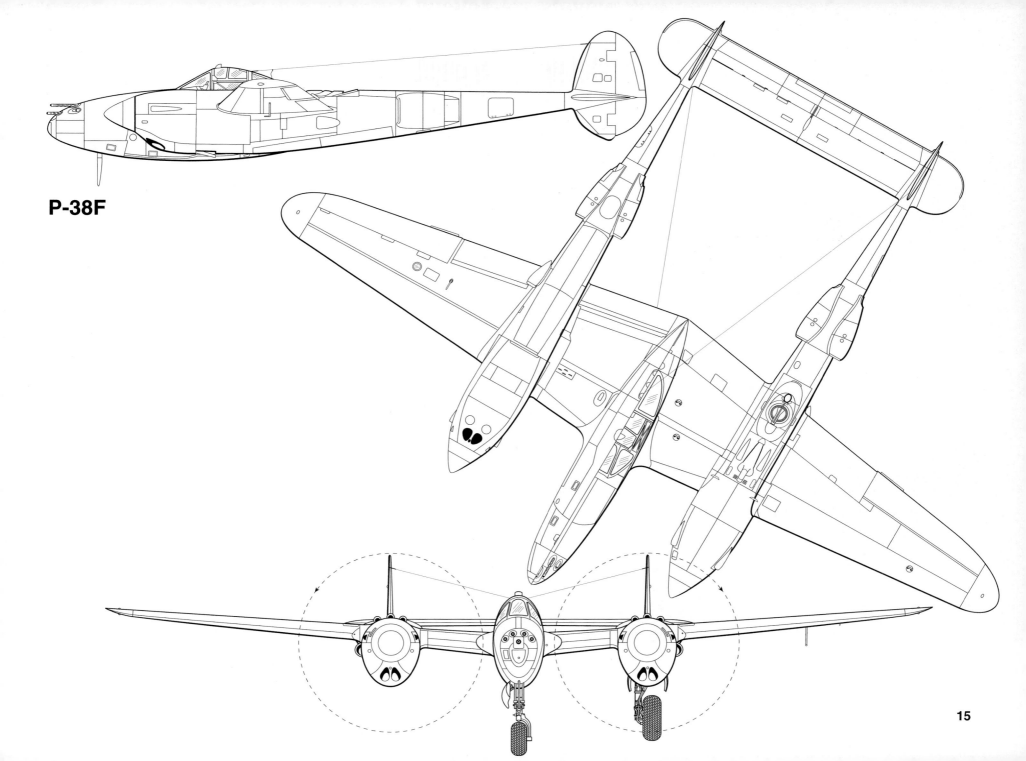

P-38F

15

An early P-38F (41-2308) assigned to the 20th FG warms up its engines at March Field, California in 1943. Its pilot steps into the cockpit while a mechanic watches from off the port wing. The side-opening canopy was unusual on a P-38F, which usually had an aft-hinged canopy. There is additional bracing on the aft cockpit glass, which was deleted during Lightning production. The distinctive pattern of the supercharger exhausts is dis-played atop the tail booms. Two Orange Yellow stripes on the aft booms indicate the B Flight commander's aircraft. The 20th FG was based at March from January to August of 1943, when it deployed to Kings Cliffe, England for service with the 8th Air Force (AF). (USAF)

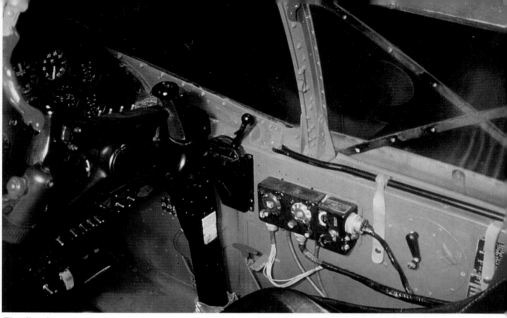

Throttles and lighting controls are placed along the port forward side wall of the P-38J cockpit. Large yellow balls top the throttle levers, while smaller black handled levers controlled propeller pitch. The landing gear lever is mounted below the throttles along the quadrant's wall. The elevator trim wheel is mounted alongside the console housing ordnance release and armament controls. (Author)

The P-38J and later variants employed a 'figure eight' type control wheel instead of the semicircular wheel on earlier Lightnings. Handgrips were mounted on the ends, while the red gun trigger was placed beside the port grip. P-38 pilots used the rudder pedals for operating the two rudders and for braking the aircraft while landing and taxiing. (Author)

The flap lever is mounted along the starboard cockpit side wall beside the control column. Radio controls are located on three black boxes aft of the flap lever. These controls allowed the pilot to select the type of radio and frequency to use during a mission. The small black hand crank opened and closed the starboard side canopy window; a similar crank for the port window was located along the port cockpit side wall. (Author)

A hydraulic oil tank is located in the port rear corner of the P-38E cockpit; this tank was also found in other Lightning variants. This tank held liquid used for the flight control systems. The hump in the cockpit floor accommodated the retracted nose wheel. Early Lightnings had cockpit walls painted Interior Green, while later aircraft used the Chromate Yellow Primer employed for all aircraft internal spaces. (Via John Clements)

17

The aft-hinged canopy is opened on this P-38F, while a mechanic sits in the cockpit. This Lightning is equipped with an N-9 reflector gun sight under the armored windshield. The sight was mounted directly to the upper edge of the instrument panel coaming. The N-9 was used on most Lightning variants through the P-38L. Additionally, a manual ring sight was provided to use in the event the reflecting sight failed. (Lockheed)

The pilot's seat installed on the same P-38G is a multi-piece unit. A .25 inch (0.6 CM) thick armor plate is mounted on the inner aft seat bucket, while another .25 inch thick plate is located between the wall and the seat. Fuse boxes were located aft along the cockpit wall. (USAFM)

The seat has been removed from this P-38G (43-2337) revealing the port side cockpit wall. The port side window crank is mounted below the window sill, with lighting controls located in the box immediately forward of this crank. Fuel tank selector controls are located atop the lower port cockpit wall console, below the lighting controls. Throttle and propeller pitch control levers top the throttle quadrant, while the landing gear control is located along this console's aft wall. (USAFM)

The circuit breaker box is mounted along the P-38G's starboard cockpit wall, immediately aft of the control column. Radio controls were placed in black boxes below and aft of the circuit breakers, while the starboard side window crank is mounted further aft. The control lock bar lying atop the cockpit wall was removed during flight. (USAFM)

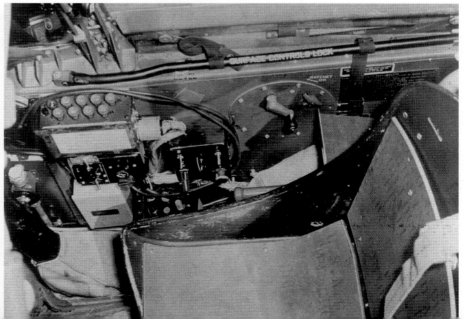

Removing the pilot's seat reveals the P-38G's cockpit floor. The nose wheel clearance bulge is located along the center of the floor. A pilot's relief tube is the slender black object draped over this wheel bulge. Piping for hydraulic liquid and oxygen and electrical wiring runs along the floor. The long handle along the starboard side is the manual hydraulic pump handle. (John Clements)

The P-38J introduced the Sperry K-14 gun sight, which replaced the earlier N-9 sight. Lightning pilots simply 'dialed in' the enemy aircraft's wingspan on the indicator aft of the NO HAND HOLD pad. The dial was mounted on the sight's port side. This same sight was also used on the North American P-51D Mustang. (USAFM)

The K-14 was mounted on a frame from the instrument panel's top and to a brace attached to the windshield frame. The angled piece of glass reflected the sight display at the pilot's eye level. The P-38J replaced the curved windshield center section and separate bulletproof plate with a flat bulletproof center section. The quarterlight panels and other canopy sections were made from Plexiglas. (USAFM)

The first P-38L (44-23769) was fitted with the older N-9 gun sight for the aircraft's trials. This is believed to be due to the shortage of K-14 sights at the time. The cockpit coaming offered some shading of the instrument panel from outside light. This allowed the pilot to easily read the instruments in flight. Foam rubber padding lined the coaming to offer some protection in the event of an accident. (Lockheed)

Most early P-38s had hubcaps fitted to the nose landing gear wheel to keep dirt out of the wheel. Many Lightnings – including this P-38J – had this cap fitted only to the port side, where the gear strut connected with the wheel. The 27 inch (68.6 см) diameter tire had a diamond shaped tread pattern, which was one of the most common tread patterns used. Lack of hydraulic pressure resulted in full compression of the oleo (shock absorbing) inner strut. (Author)

Most later P-38 variants dispensed with the nose wheel hub cap to reduce production and maintenance time. This P-38J is fitted with the circumferential tread design tire that was an alternate to the diamond shaped tread. The chrome plated oleo strut is exposed due to sufficient hydraulic pressure. The red painted tow hook below the oleo was used for towing the Lightning on the ground. (Keith Melville)

(Above) The P-38 nose gear door had four hinges to starboard and was bulged at the rear for tire clearance. The nose gear fully retracted aft into the gear bay. The gear bay and door interior on this restored P-38J is painted ANA 611 Interior Green (FS34151); however, factory specifications called for Chromate Yellow Primer to be used on these areas. (Keith Melville)

(Right) The forward bulkhead of the gear bay mounted the nose landing gear strut pivot points. Two retraction struts flanked the main gear strut and pulled the gear up and aft into the bay. Hydraulic lines for the gear and door run along the forward bulkhead. This restored P-38's nose gear bay and door interior is painted Aluminum (FS17178). (Author)

The nose gear door was opened using a hydraulic strut mounted on the aft gear bay bulkhead. Pipes carried hydraulic liquid from the storage tank in the cockpit to the landing gear struts and doors. The nose wheel clearance bulge was placed in the bay's ceiling, which also served as the cockpit floor. The canvas strap across the bay opening was used for this restoration effort and was not found on operational P-38s. (Keith Melville)

Workbenches and ammunition bins flank the nose of this P-38D undergoing tests at Lockheed's Burbank plant. The four .50 caliber weapons were mounted high on the nose. Early Lightnings were also armed with a 37MM Browning M9 cannon, which was replaced by a 20MM Bendix M1 weapon on the P-38E. A gun camera was mounted in the lower nose below the cannon until it was moved to the port wing pylon on the P-38J. (Lockheed)

A Lockheed armorer pushes a loaded 500-round .50 caliber ammunition canister back into position. The small rotary 'drum' on the workbench was a 150-round 20MM ammunition canister. Both the gun bay door interiors and the ammunition bins were natural metal, while the gun bay itself was painted Chromate Yellow Primer. A rod extended from the aft bay section kept the inward-hinged gun bay doors opened for servicing. (Lockheed)

A Lockheed technician fires the P-38F's four nose-mounted .50 caliber (12.7MM) Browning M2 machine guns on a nighttime ground test. This mounting resulted in an almost nonexistent spray pattern to the guns and a high percentage of hits. The wing fillet added to this Lightning variant eliminated elevator buffeting that troubled earlier P-38s. The rear view mirror fitted to all production Lightnings protrudes from atop the canopy. (Lockheed)

2/Lt John A. MacKay (right) points to the tail of a Messerschmitt Bf 109 he shot down flying his P-38G, *Shoot..YOU'RE FADED* (42-13417), on 25 May 1943. The German aircraft was the fifth 'kill' for MacKay, who was assigned to the 27th FS, 1st FG at Chatteaudun-du-Rhumel, Algeria. (Lockheed)

Two 339th FS ground crew examine a crashed P-38 on Vella Lavella in the Solomons in October of 1943. The port gun bay door was opened when the guns and ammunition bins were removed from the Lightning. This aircraft was then stripped of all usable parts and abandoned. The 339th FS was assigned to the 347th FG. (USAF)

Lockheed armament technicians load .50 caliber ammunition belts into an ammunition bin on a P-38J in 1944. Metal links held the rounds together until they were chambered and fired from the weapon. Each .50 caliber ammunition canister held a total of 500 rounds. Expended ammunition casings were ejected through small chutes cut into the nose undersurface. (Lockheed)

P-38Hs assigned to the 55th FS, 20th FG are parked at Wittering, England in late 1943 or early 1944. The 55th FG was one of only three 8th AF fighter groups to fly the P-38 before transitioning into P-51 Mustangs in mid-1944. A Lockheed presentation marking derived from its winged star emblem is painted on the near aircraft's nose. (USAFM)

The typical data block of the P-38 contained the aircraft type and block number (P-38J-10), manufacturer (-LO for Lockheed), serial number, (42-67855), maximum recommended crew weight (200 pounds/90.7 KG), and other pertinent service information. The white cross marking indicated this Lightning had 62 gallon (234.7 L) wing leading edge fuel tanks installed. It was not the center of gravity marking on a P-38. (Author)

The P-38-LO through P-38J had a gun camera mounted in the nose. This motion picture camera recorded the results of firing runs for confirmation of victories and tactical study. Access to this device was through the opened nose cap, which was hinged to starboard. The P-38L had the gun camera moved to the port wing pylon, where it was less prone to blurred pictures. (John Clements)

An elevator flutter problem developed during flight testing of early P-38 variants. The P-38E and all subsequent models had the wing-to-fuselage joint modified with a large fairing and forward extension of the wing leading edge. This fillet smoothed the airflow over the elevator and eliminated the buffet. (Keith Melville)

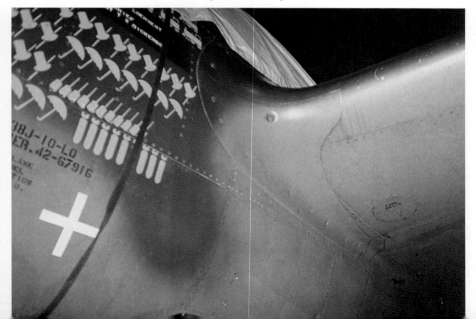

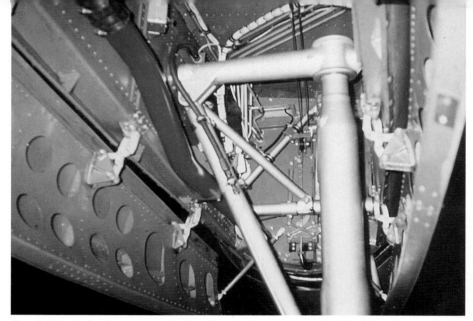

The P-38 main landing gear and retraction struts were mounted into the main gear bay's front section. Aluminum hydraulic pipes run along the gear bay walls and ceiling. Lightening holes were cut into the sheet metal cover for the gear doors' inner surfaces as a weight saving measure. (Keith Melville)

The main landing gear bay ceiling had a small step in the center, where the bay height was reduced. The oval indentation provided clearance for the main wheel. The thick blue pipe carried engine coolant towards the aft-mounted radiators. Lockheed painted the gear bays and door interiors Chromate Yellow Primer for anti-corrosion protection. (Keith Melville)

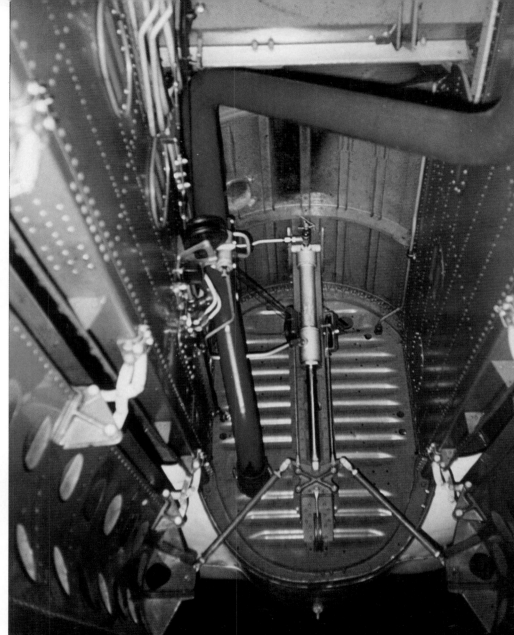

A hydraulic cylinder for the main landing gear door actuators is mounted on the aft gear bay bulkhead. Two actuators aft work with a pair mounted forward to open and close the gear doors. Each main gear door has five hinges connecting it to the tail boom. Engine coolant was fed through the blue pipe to the radiator, which is located immediately aft of the gear bay bulkhead. (Keith Melville)

(Above Left) A 431st FS, 475th FG P-38F (132) is parked on 12 Mile Strip near Port Moresby, New Guinea in August of 1943. This Lightning – the first operational fighter aircraft with tricycle landing gear – has a greater nose-high 'stance' on the ground, due to having its nose-mounted guns and ammunition removed. The 475th FG was the top scoring P-38 unit during the war, recording 540 victories between 16 August 1943 and 28 March 1945. (Vincent Straus)

(Above) A P-38G (138) assigned to the 339th FS, 347th FG rests at Fighter 2 airstrip on Guadalcanal, the Solomon Islands in late 1943. The P-38G was virtually identical to all previous variants with the exception of the installation of upgraded 1325 HP V-1710-51/55 engines. Lockheed built 1462 P-38Gs, of which 180 were modified to F-5A photo-reconnaissance aircraft. (US Marine Corps)

(Left) A US Navy PBY Catalina pilot stands beside Phoebe (122) a P-38G-13-LO (43-2338) at Fighter 2 airfield on Guadalcanal. This was the Lightning flown by Capt Tom Lanphier of the 339th FS, 347th FG. On 18 April 1943, 16 P-38s of this Squadron flew from Guadalcanal to the coast of Bougainville. The fighters successfully intercepted the Mitsubishi G4M (Betty) bomber carrying Admiral Isoruku Yamamoto, Commander-in-Chief of the Japanese Combined Fleet. Both Lanphier and 1/Lt Rex Barber claimed credit for shooting down Yamamoto's aircraft, but Lanphier was officially awarded full credit for the 'kill.' The nose wheel has been removed from its strut. (John Stanaway)

(Above) *Monica III* was a P-38H assigned to the 94th FS, 1st FG at Salsola Airfield, Italy, in early 1944. The P-38H was powered by two V-1710-89/91, which were each rated at 1425 HP at 25,000 feet (7620 M). Lightnings of the 94th FS had Orange Yellow propeller spinners and 'command stripes' on the aft nacelles. The Squadron's code letters UN are painted in white on the aft nacelle radiator housing, followed by the individual aircraft letter, which is believed to be a B. (Via Keith Melville)

(Above Right) Capt Tommy McGuire stands next to a P-38H (164) on the ramp at Port Moresby in late 1943 or early 1944. He was assigned to the 431st FS, 475th FG. The aircraft carries the standard 300 gallon (1135.6 L) Lockheed-designed underwing drop tanks, which were introduced on the earlier P-38G. This Lightning is equipped with block treaded tires. (Author's Collection)

(Right) Lockheed combined two photographs to show armorers how to load bombs aboard a P-38's wing pylons. The near image shows someone lifting a 1100 pound (499 KG) bomb using a hoist directly attached to the pylon. The far photo shows the bomb mounted on the pylon and the hoist removed. The dummy weapon used for this demonstration lacks the fusing wires attached to actual bombs. The propeller mounted on the bomb's nose armed the weapon after it had fallen a set distance from the aircraft. (Lockheed)

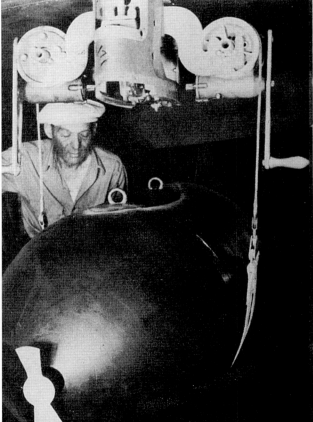

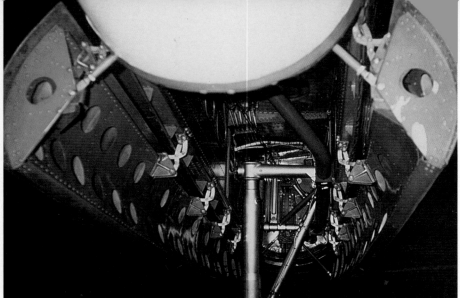

Actuator rods are fitted to both the forward and aft main landing gear door bulkheads. Five pairs of hinges connect the doors to the tail booms. Lightening holes are cut into the gear door inner surfaces, but this was not always the case with some P-38s. The main landing gear strut retracted aft into the gear bay. Although the gear bay and door interiors are Interior Green, the gear strut is left in natural metal. (Keith Melville)

The forward gear door actuator rod attachment section was smaller than the one fitted to the aft door bulkhead. This P-38's gear door inner surfaces lack the lightening holes put in the door interiors of other Lightnings. Lips around the door edges ensure a flush fit with the tail boom when the gear is retracted. Two hydraulic lines run down along the main landing gear strut. (Author)

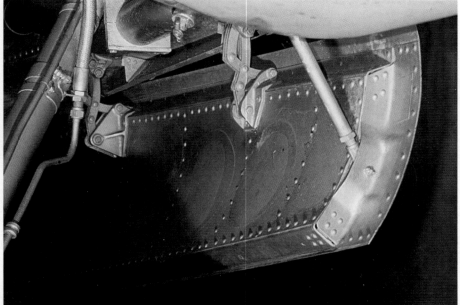

A plate was bolted over the main landing gear door actuator mechanism and hydraulic cylinder on the US Air Force Museum's P-38J. This item was only fitted to some Lightnings; most aircraft lacked this plate to save on maintenance. Actuator rods are attached from the door actuator to the aft gear door edges. The thick coolant pipe carries engine coolant aft to the radiator immediately behind the gear bay bulkhead. This restored P-38J's gear bay interior is painted Aluminum, rather than the factory standard Chromate Yellow Primer. (Author)

The P-38J's main landing gear featured a single inboard-mounted main strut. A scissor link connected the main strut with the wheel axle attachment and the shock-absorbing oleo strut within the main strut. This oleo was chromed for ease of movement within the main strut. A hydraulic hose runs around the scissor link to the main wheel. Bendix disc brakes were installed on the main wheels, which were fitted inside 36 inch (91.4 cm) diameter tires. (Author)

Early P-38s had outboard main wheel hubcaps fitted to keep dirt out of the brakes. Later aircraft had this cap removed to expose the spoked wheel, which allowed air to cool the disc brakes. Yellow rectangles were painted on the wheel and tire edges to mark their proper alignment. The tire inflation stem juts out of the wheel opening below the strut. This P-38J was equipped with circumferential tread pattern main tires. (Author)

Another P-38J under restoration is fitted with the circumferential tread pattern tires, which were common on Lightnings. Main gear struts were left in natural metal at the factory, with the oleos chromed for ease of movement. The scissor strut is in a normal position for a lightly loaded P-38 on the ground. This strut compressed with greater weight placed on it and extended with weight taken off it. Wheel chocks placed fore and aft kept the wheel secure while the aircraft was on the ground. The red pan collected leaking hydraulic liquid. (Keith Melville)

The 50th P-38J-10-LO (42-67452) is parked on the ramp at Lockheed's Burbank plant in late 1943 or early 1944. The P-38J was the first Lightning variant equipped with the pronounced 'chin' under the propellers. This 'chin' housed enlarged air intakes for the oil coolers, which were mounted on the wing leading edges in earlier P-38 variants. The Lockheed factory number (1963) on the nose is Neutral Gray, while part of a white W is painted on the nose and another white W appears on the radiator housing. The purpose of this code letter is unknown. (Lockheed)

Three columns of P-38Js undergo final assembly at Burbank in August of 1944. The flaps are fully lowered during this stage of production, when there is no hydraulic pressure on these surfaces. Dark covers placed over the wings prevent the shoes of workers and mechanics from scuffing the natural metal surface. The USAAF ended the requirement for camouflaging most new production combat aircraft in August of 1943. (Lockheed)

Lockheed Chief Test Pilot Tony LeVier stands on a P-38L at Chico Army Air Field (AAF), California in 1944. He is explaining the differences between this aircraft and all previous P-38 variants. The P-38J and P-38L were almost identical except for the movement of the landing light from inside the outer wing panel to the port wing leading edge. LeVier later put on a flying demonstration of the P-38L, which left all the troops in awe. (Lockheed)

LeVier stands in front of a brand new P-38L-5-LO (722/44-53078) on Lockheed's Burbank ramp in 1944. Guns were not mounted on this Lightning and covers were placed over their openings in the nose. A highly polished oval mirror was mounted on the inboard engine nacelles, just below the antiglare panel. The pilot used this mirror to check the nose landing gear status. P-38Ls had the gun camera moved from the lower nose to the port wing pylon leading edge. (Lockheed)

A mechanic services the starboard V-1710 engine of an 8th FG P-38J at the 21st Air Depot facility on Morotai, Netherlands East Indies (now Indonesia) in 1945. Engine cowling panels were removed to service the Allison powerplant, which was overhauled at the depot level every 100 flight hours. Large ducts for the intercooler and carburetor intakes run along the nacelle sides and under the wing leading edge. (Lockheed)

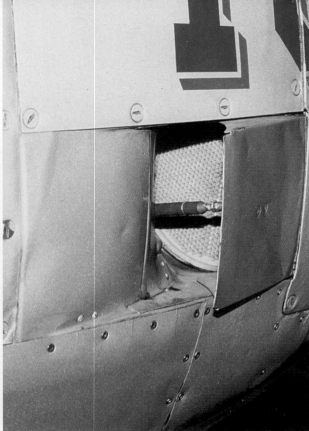

(Above Left) Engine panels are removed from this P-38J undergoing restoration at the Fighter Collection at Duxford, England. An Allison V-1710-89 engine was mounted on the P-38J's port nacelle, while a V-1710-91 was located to starboard. These engines were identical apart from the gear box, which allowed the propeller to turn in opposite directions. Fully-feathering Curtiss Electric propellers replaced Hamilton Standard propellers during P-38E production. These propellers were either 'left handed' or 'right handed' for installation on the port or starboard engines, respectively. The exhaust manifold in the upper nacelle ducted gasses to the turbo-superchargers. Oil radiator exhaust ducts were mounted along the lower nacelle. (Keith Melville)

(Above) A small air exhaust flap is mounted on both the inboard and outboard engine nacelle sides. Excess air from the oil radiator inlet is vented out through the spring-mounted door. This door closes when there is no excess air to vent. The adjoining access panels are secured to the nacelle using flush-mounted Dzus fasteners. (Author)

(Left) The starboard propeller spinner and engine access panels are removed from this P-38J. The propeller hub enclosed the pitch adjustment controls, which set the blades at angles ranging from 22.7° for normal flight to 87.5° for full feathering. Engine support accessories were placed in the aft engine cowling section, whose access panel was located in front of and under the wing leading edge. (John Clements)

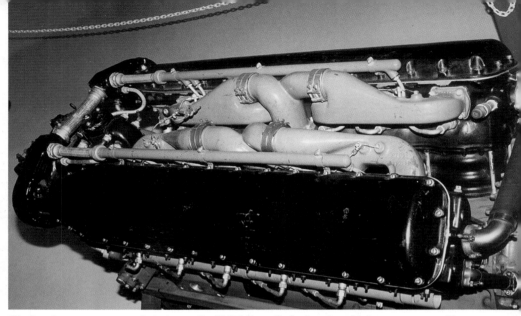

P-38s were powered by variants of the Allison V-1710 F series 12-cylinder, liquid-cooled, V-engine. It was designed in 1931 and became the world's first 1000 HP inline engine four years later. The V-1710 also powered the Bell P-39 Airacobra, the Curtiss P-40 Warhawk, and the North American P-51A Mustang. This V-1710 E is from a P-39, but is similar in configuration to the Lightning's V-1710 F series. (Author)

Black valve covers were placed over the V-1710's cylinder heads, which were arranged in two rows of six cylinders. The gray manifold carried the engine exhaust aft to the turbo-supercharger. The V-1710's power output increased from the 1150 HP in the P-38D's V-1710-27/29 to 1475 HP in the P-38L's V-1710-111/113. (Author)

Access panels removed from this P-38J undergoing restoration reveal various liquid pipes servicing the V-1710 engine. The black tube running along the side was an engine-bearing frame, which helped secure the powerplant to the airframe. A small scoop on the upper side directed cooling air over the exhaust manifold. This scoop was located on both the port and starboard nacelle sides. (John Clements)

A Curtiss Electric C532D propeller is removed with part of its spinner from a P-38J. The three-bladed metal propeller was a constant speed, selective pitch unit which used electrical power for adjusting the blades' pitch in flight or on the ground. The gear at the base fitted into the V-1710's gearbox, which turned the propeller at its proper speed. The Curtiss Electric C532D had a diameter of 11 feet 6 inches (3.5 M). (John Clements)

33

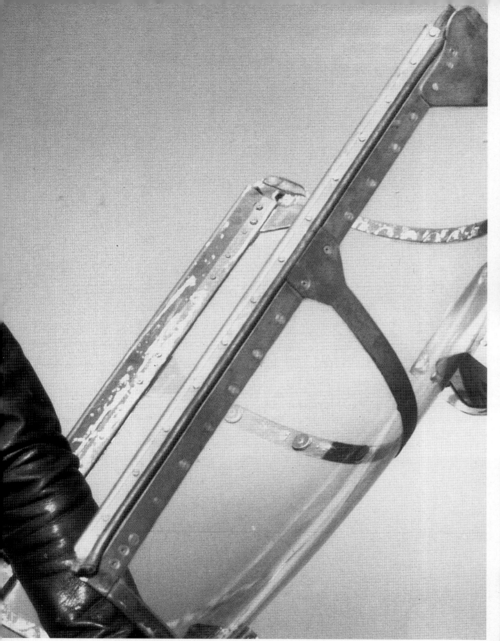

A 474th FG ground crew prepares to install new V-1710 engines in a 429th FS P-38J (7Y-T). This occurred on the snow covered ramp at Florennes, Belgium during the winter of 1944-45. A chain hoist mounted on a frame was used to help remove old engines and to help install new V-1710s. Silver paint was brushed over the black and white Normandy Invasion stripes under the wings. (James V. Crow)

Personnel rearm a 36th FS, 8th FG P-38J (N) on the ramp at Ie Shima, near Okinawa, in mid-1945. Two armorers – one each to port and starboard of the nose – stand on wooden work platforms while loading the .50 caliber (12.7mm) ammunition belts. Steel hydraulic work platforms were not available to combat squadron at most stations during the war. (James V Crow)

The P-38F introduced an aft-hinged cockpit canopy, which replaced the side-hinged unit installed on earlier Lightning variants. This canopy opened up and aft, going past the hinge point's center. A thin metal reinforcement band was wrapped around the center section. The rear view mirror was enclosed within a small Plexiglas bubble atop the canopy. All P-38 canopies used manual operation. (USAFM)

The pilot's entrance ladder is lowered on this rather scruffy P-38. A crewman used the lever on the upper aft center section to raise or lower the ladder. From this ladder, the pilot walked along the inboard wing surface to the cockpit. The Lightning's inboard flaps are fully lowered without hydraulic pressure on them. (John Clements)

Tracks within the inboard flap bays guided the P-38's inboard Fowler Flap. The flap was removed for maintenance and to reveal the flap well. Hydraulically activated struts attached to the flaps fitted within the tracks. Each Lightning had two inboard and two outboard flaps for additional wing area on take off and landing. (John Clements)

With everything 'down and dirty,' a 35th FS, 8th FG P-38L-5-LO (X/44-26869) returns to Ie Shima following a mission in mid-1945. The Squadron's Lightnings had spinners, wing bands, and tail tip in yellow with black trim. All P-38s had Fowler Flaps, which increased wing area during operation by sliding out of the lower side of the wing. The flap moved aft to the trailing edge before deflecting into the air stream. (James V Crow)

The flap well was located before the trailing edge of the P-38's wing. Structural ribs were mounted in the well ceiling. This ceiling formed the lower section of the fuel tank storage area in the Lightning's inboard wing surfaces. Flap wells were usually finished in Zinc Chromate Primer. (John Clements)

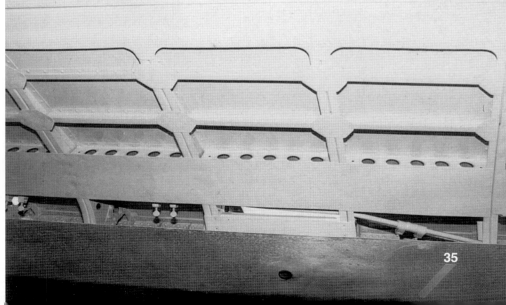

The starboard Curtiss Electric C532D propeller is fully feathered on this P-38J at Duxford, England. A pilot usually employed this 87.5° setting when the engine was out. Placing the propeller blades into a 'knife-edge' direction into the air stream prevented the propeller from 'windmilling,' which resulted in unnecessary drag upon the aircraft. From late 1941, P-38 propeller blades were Flat Black (FS37038) with Flat Orange Yellow (FS33538) tips. (Keith Melville)

Curtiss Electric propeller decals were applied onto factory fresh P-38s, approximately halfway down the length of each blade. This decal and the surrounding blade surface display some signs of wear. Most propeller decals were removed in combat by the high propeller speeds, weather, or environmental conditions, especially in the Pacific Theatre. (Via John Clements)

This decal near the propeller hub displays the specifications for its installation in Orange Yellow letters. The three angles of propeller settings – low (22.7°), high (57.7°), and feathering (87.5°) – are also given for the benefit of maintenance crews. This information was displayed on each propeller blade. (Via John Clements)

A propeller blade partially obscures the air intakes on this P-38J. The central intake fed the intercooler radiator, while the flanking openings fed air into the oil cooler. A mesh screen fitted to the oil cooler kept out most foreign objects, although some dirt and sand did get into this cooler. This air intake arrangement was standard on P-38J and later variants. (Author)

A turbo-supercharger intake is mounted on the outboard engine boom, forward of the radiator. This scoop was found on both port and starboard booms. Air was collected through this intake and fed into the turbo-supercharger. The P-38J introduced a larger round intake opening, which replaced the smaller oval opening on earlier Lightning variants. (Author)

The hydraulically-actuated oil cooler air vent door is opened on the port inboard nacelle. This and an identical door on the outboard side allowed excess air from the oil cooler to vent from the engine bay interior. This measure regulated oil temperatures within the engine bay. The opened door reveals the oil radiator. The pilot used the highly polished oval panel above this door to check on the nose landing gear's condition for landing. (Author)

The turbo-supercharger intake has a streamlined teardrop shape, with it flaring to a point on the aft end. This scoop caused little aerodynamic drag on the Lightning. Air coming through this intake was ducted up and through the main landing gear well and into the turbo-supercharger, which was mounted atop the engine boom. (Author)

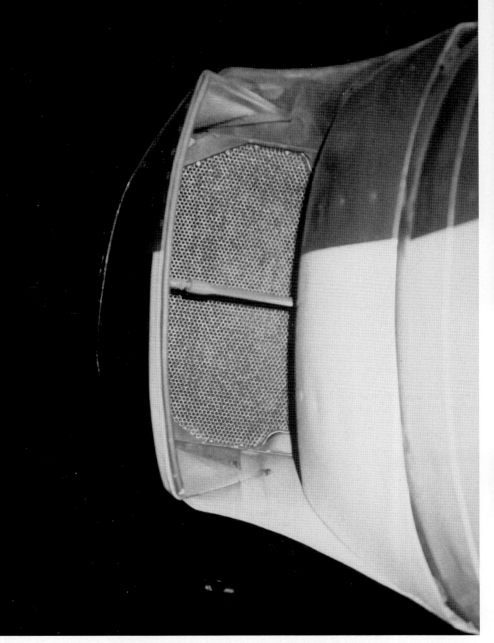

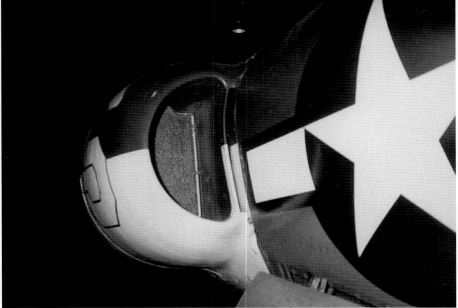

Engine radiator intakes flanked both engine boom sides immediately aft of the main landing gear bay. The semi-circular openings collected air for cooling the radiator, where heated engine coolant was circulated. An anti-foreign object screen is placed inside the intake. P-38Js and later variants featured radiators which were larger, yet more aerodynamically efficient than those fitted to earlier Lightnings. (Keith Melville)

This P-38's engine coolant radiator exhaust door is in the normal closed position for flight. The pilot opened and closed this door hydraulically from the cockpit as conditions warranted. Fully closed, the door provided a fairly tight aerodynamic seal on this aft radiator section, which aided its streamlining qualities. (Author)

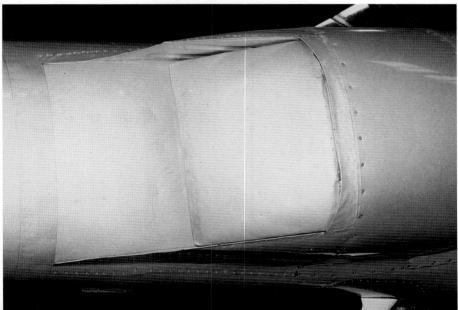

The engine coolant radiator exhaust doors are opened on this statically-displayed P-38. A hydraulic actuator closed the door in flight and opened it while on the ground. A mesh screen covered the radiator exhaust opening to keep out foreign objects, which would otherwise interfere with efficient operation. This opening was found on both the inboard and outboard nacelle sides. (Keith Melville)

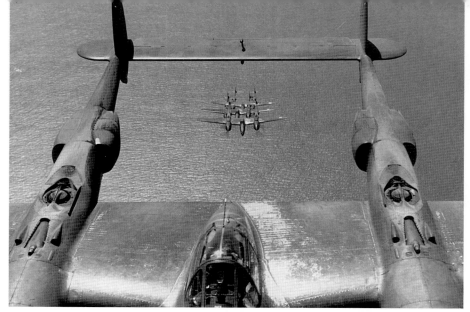

A flight of 95th FS P-38s fly over the Mediterranean Sea in early to mid-1943. The upper wing surfaces display a wear pattern on the paint caused by crew members walking on the inner wing. Exhaust staining on the upper portion of the aft engine nacelles behind the supercharger exhausts was typical of all P-38s. The 95th FS was assigned to the 82nd FG, 12th Air Force during this time. (Lockheed)

Sgt Harry Kawaski, a 347th FG armorer, stands by *The Lords Prayer*, an early P-38J assigned to the Group's 339th FS on Leyte, the Philippines in early 1945. This Lightning is equipped with 165 gallon (624.6 L) underwing drop tanks, which were commonly carried by all P-38s in the Pacific Theatre. The color of the nose trim and propeller spinners is unknown. (Richard Schulenberg)

P-38 designer Clarence L. 'Kelly' Johnson (left) and Lockheed chief test pilot Milo Burcham discuss the new compressibility or dive recovery flaps just above their heads. Burcham's hand gestures showed Johnson what happens when these electrically-operated flaps were deployed. The dive flaps were introduced on the P-38J-25-LO and were standard on subsequent variants. They restored lift to P-38s that otherwise stalled and became uncontrollable, particularly at low altitude. The dive flaps reached 35° deflection in only one second. (Lockheed)

(Above) The Fighter Collection's P-38J (NX3145) is pulled out of its hangar at Duxford, England prior to its first flight in the spring of 1992. Fighter Rebuilders – located at the Planes of Fame Museum in Chino, California – restored the Lightning to airworthy condition before shipment to Britain in March of 1992. It was painted in the markings of California Cutie, a P-38J-10-LO (KI-S/42-67543) flown by 1/Lt Richard Loehnert. He was assigned to 55th Fighter Squadron (FS), 20th Fighter Group (FG), 8th Air Force (AF) at Kings Cliffe, England in mid-1944. The Lightning was camouflaged with Olive Drab (FS34087) upper surfaces and Neutral Gray (FS36173) undersurfaces. Black and white invasion stripes for the assault on northern France (Operation OVER-LORD) were painted on the wings and tail booms. This P-38J was destroyed in an airshow accident at Duxford on 14 July 1996, which killed the pilot, Michael 'Hoof' Proudfoot. (Keith Melville)

(Left) California Cutie's port gun bay door is slightly opened while the P-38J sits in its hangar in Duxford. Paint was removed from the nose and it was highly polished, while a white band was painted immediately aft of it. This simulated the Plexiglas nose of P-38 'Droop Snoot' bomber aircraft assigned to the 20th FG. The 56 top hat and cane combinations painted on the nose represented escort missions Lt Loehnert's P-38 flew during World War Two. Top cover missions were represented by the 16 umbrellas, fighter sweeps by the 11 brooms, and the six locomotives were destroyed on strafing missions. The white cross on the lower nose indicated the installation of outer wing leading edge fuel tanks in this Lightning. Loehnert had two aerial victories – a pair of Bf 109s downed on 7 July 1944. (Keith Melville)

The P-38J was armed with four .50 caliber (12.7MM) Browning M2 machine guns with 500 rounds per gun. They were arrayed over the 20MM Bendix M1 cannon, which was a license-built version of France's Hispano-Suiza 404 weapon. The cannon was supplied with 150 rounds of High Explosive Incendiary (HEI) and Armor Piercing Tracer (APT) ammunition. (Author)

A forward-looking gun camera was moved from the lower nose to the port underwing pylon beginning on the P-38L variant. This installation allowed photos to be taken without vibration from gun firing, which resulted in blurred images. Various access panels for electrical connections and fuel plumbing are fitted to the pylon surface. (Author)

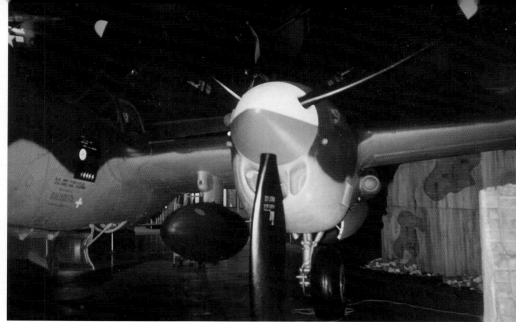

A 165 gallon (624.6 L) drop tank is mounted on the port wing pylon of this restored P-38L-5-LO (44-53232). This Lightning is on display at the US Air Force Museum at Wright-Patterson Air Force Base in Dayton, Ohio. A gun camera is mounted on the leading edge of the wing pylon. The anti-compressibility dive flap is mounted on the outboard wing undersurface. (Author)

Fuel tanks, bombs, and other ordnance were fitted onto two hooks in the pylon's under-surface. These hooks engaged lifting lugs mounted on the item. The starboard underwing pylon was identical to the port pylon, but lacked the forward-mounted gun camera. Late P-38 underwing pylons normally held up to 1600 pounds (725.8 KG) of ordnance, although 2000 pounds (907.2 KG) was not out of the ordinary. (Author)

P-38M

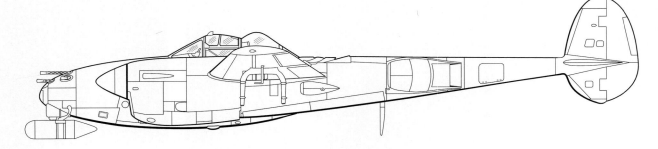

F-5B
(Nose Profile)

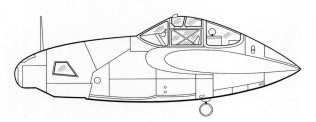

F-5E
(Nose Profile)

F-5G
(Nose Profile)

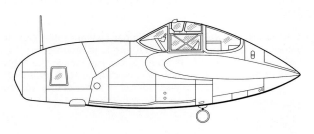

P-38J 'Droop Snoot'
(Nose Profile)

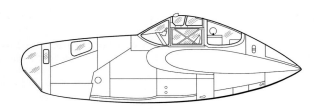

Lockheed P-38J Lightning Specifications

Wingspan:................52 feet (15.8 м)
Length:....................37 feet 10 inches (11.5 м)
Height:.....................9 feet 10 inches (3 м)
Empty Weight:........12,780 pounds (5797 кg)
Maximum Weight:..17,500 pounds (7938 кg)
Powerplant:............Two 1600 нр Allison V-1710-89/91 12-cylinder, liquid-cooled, inline engines

Armament:..............One 20мм M1 cannon with 150 rounds and four .50 caliber (12.7мм) M2 machine guns with 500 rounds per gun in the nose. Up to 4000 pounds (1814.4 кg) of ordnance carried under the wings.

Performance:
  Maximum Speed:.421 мрн (677.5 кмн) at 25,000 feet (7620 м)
  Service Ceiling:....44,000 feet (13,411.2 м)
  Range:....................2100 miles (3379.5 км)
Crew:.......................One

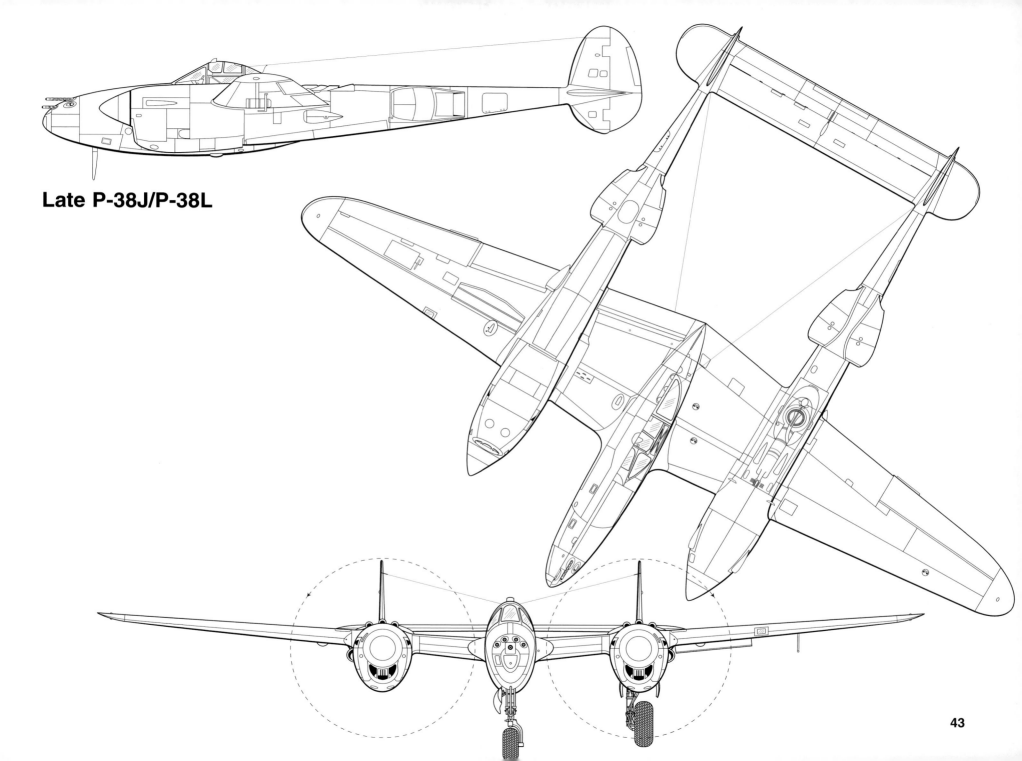

Late P-38J/P-38L

43

(Above) The inboard Fowler Flap is fully extended on this P-38. Each of the four flaps – two inboard and two outboard – was attached to the wing using two positioning arms and two parallel actuating rods. These rods fit inside tracks located on the flap well sides. The pilot controlled the hydraulically-operated flaps from the cockpit. The inboard wing flaps were 5 feet 9.25 inches (1.8 м) wide, while the outboard flaps measured 5 feet 1.25 inches (1.6 м) in width. (Via John Clements)

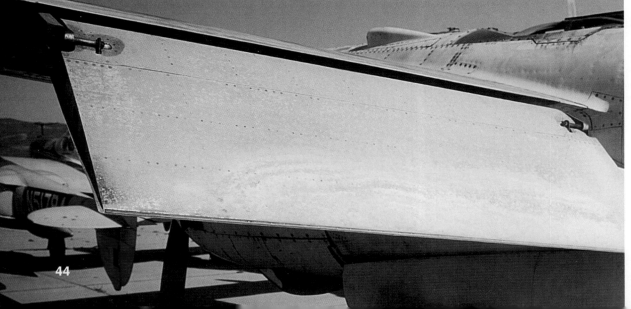

(Left) Hinges for the wing flaps were mounted on the forward upper surface corners. These hinges were connected to the positioning arms and actuator rods that moved the flaps aft and down on extension, or forward and up on retraction. The flaps were flush with the upper wing surface when fully retracted. (Via John Clements)

This P-38's starboard outer wing flap is fully extended. Both positioning arms are mounted above the bay well tracks where the actuating rods fit. Ribs and cross braces were fitted into the flap bay ceiling for strength. This bay was painted Chromate Yellow Primer (FS33481) at the factory, although this restored Lightning has the area painted in a gray. (John Clements)

The positioning arms moved the Fowler Flap aft on extension, while the actuator rods angled this flap into the air stream. Four lightening holes were cut into the port outer flap well support rib. The port aileron is mounted just outboard of this flap. (John Clements)

Flap interior surfaces were painted Chromate Yellow Primer at the factory to prevent corrosion. This color was normally used for the flap bay; however, this restored P-38's flap well is painted the same Neutral Gray as the undersurface color. The pilot adjusted a trim tab protruding from the port aileron. This allowed the aileron to maintain a proper neutral position in level flight. (Detail & Scale Photo by Bert Kinzey)

A P-38J-10-LO (42-68071) is parked on a US airfield in western Europe in late 1944. It has retained the 24 inch (61 CM) wide invasion stripes painted for the Allied assault on France (Operation OVERLORD) on 6 June 1944. Three white and two black stripes were painted on the tail booms and wings to prevent Allied gunners firing on the Lightning by mistake, despite the P-38's highly distinctive outline. Light gray paint was put on the white sections of the national insignia to reduce its visibility to German fighter pilots. (Art Krieger)

1/Lt Carroll Anderson flew this P-38J-15-LO VIRGINIA MARIE (194/42-104508) while assigned to the 433rd FS, 475th FG at Biak Island, near New Guinea, in October of 1944. The Lightning had non-standard Light Blue (FS15102) anti-glare panels to match the propeller spinners, wing bands, and tail bands. The latter bands are trimmed in white. Anderson did not score any 'kills' during his tour of duty with the 433rd FS. (Author's Collection)

D-Day Invasion Stripes Pattern
(Split Plan View)

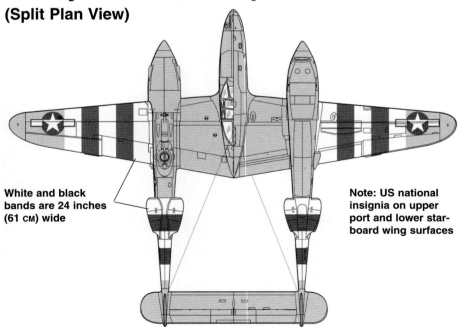

White and black bands are 24 inches (61 CM) wide

Note: US national insignia on upper port and lower starboard wing surfaces

TWICKS JAYHAWKER/GINNY JEAN was a P-38L-5-LO (103/44-26199) assigned to the 68th FS, 347th FG at San Jose, Mindoro, the Philippines in 1945. The last four serial number digits are repeated on the nose; however, they are being worn away. The small number 423 on the nose is believed to be a Lockheed constructor's number. The Olive Drab antiglare panel on the nose kept solar glare from the pilot's eyes. The propeller spinners and the lightning bolt on the tail are Insignia Red (FS11136). Exhaust residue on the vertical tail obscures the lightning bolt and serial number. The number 103 on the radiator housing was a squadron code number. Just visible under the port wing is the retracted dive recovery flap. (James V. Crow)

KROGHAN KID was a P-38J-25-LO (7F-W) assigned to the 485th FS, 370th FG at Gutersloh, Germany in 1945. Gutersloh was one of the many airfields occupied by US and other Allied forces after Germany's surrender on 8 May 1945. Both the nose art and the propeller spinners are Insignia Blue (FS15044) and Insignia Red. The black triangle on the vertical tail indicated the Squadron. (USAFM)

Ground crew refuel a P-38J assigned to the 433rd FS, 475th FG at Dulag Air Base, Leyte, the Philippines in late 1944. Aviation gasoline is pumped from 55 gallon (208.2 L) drums into the 165 gallon (624.6 L) underwing fuel tanks. This was accomplished by forcing air into the fuel drum, which pumped the fuel into the hose. The gun barrels were plugged to keep out the incessant jungle moisture. (Author's Collection)

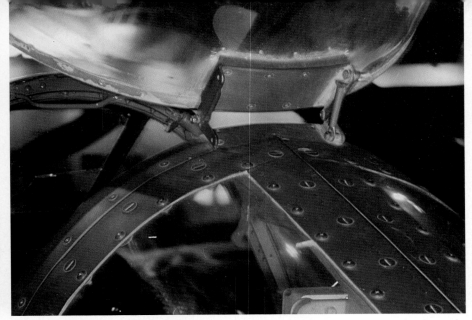

A small Plexiglas bubble for the rear view mirror was mounted atop the canopy. This bubble was located on the forward portion of the upper canopy, which was hinged aft. The pilot looked up into the mirror to track aircraft approaching from behind him. The P-38 was the first production fighter equipped with an all-around canopy. (Author)

A General Electric (GE) Type B9 turbo-supercharger was mounted atop each P-38 engine nacelle. Exhaust gas from the Allison V-1710 engine was vented aft to turn the supercharger. In turn, this forced a higher fuel-air mixture into the cylinder head, which greatly increased the engine's horsepower at high altitudes. Two small supercharger cooling intakes flank the supercharger, while the scoop at the front feeds the cockpit heater. (Author)

The upper canopy hinge was a two-arm item mounted on the aft canopy framing. The thin hinge arms protruded when the canopy was closed, but caused little aerodynamic drag. The aft-opening canopy was introduced on the P-38F, replacing the side-opening canopy fitted to earlier Lightning variants. (Author)

Exhaust from the V-1710 engine vented through the GE Type B9 turbo-supercharger out of the P-38. The turbine was located immediately forward of the exhaust port. The Type B9 raised the V-1710's output from 1090 HP in the non-supercharged P-322 to 1425 HP in the P-38J/L. Superchargers were left unpainted, due to the extreme heat in this area. The P-38 was the world's first production fighter equipped with superchargers. (Author)

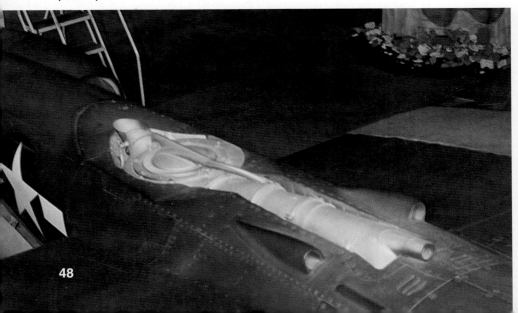

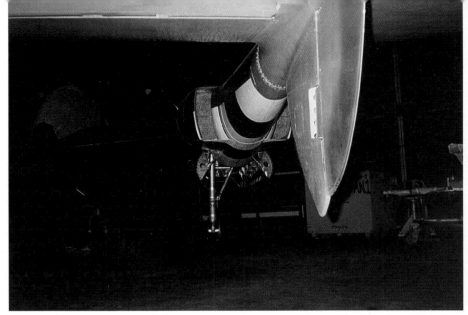

The lower starboard vertical tail surface juts from the tail boom of this restored P-38J. A reinforced point on the bottom of the vertical fin assembly offered protection in case the pilot dragged the tail on takeoff or landing. The engine radiator ducts are left open, which was normal for ground operation; these doors were usually closed during flight. A radio was mounted inside the aft starboard boom, while oxygen was housed to port. (Keith Melville)

An external mass balance is fitted to the elevator upper surface; an identical balance is located on the undersurface. Elevator vibration problems during XP-38 prototype testing resulted in these balances being added on the YP-38 service test aircraft. Although the mass balances did not cure this problem, they were incorporated into all Lightning production variants. (Author)

The P-38J's rudder was hinged above and below the horizontal stabilizer. A trim tab is fitted to the upper rudder and the pilot adjusted this as necessary from the cockpit. Lightning rudders were divided into upper and lower sections, which were linked and moved simultaneously to input from the rudder pedals. All P-38 control surfaces (rudders, elevator, and ailerons) were metal covered, instead of the fabric-covered surfaces common among World War Two-era aircraft. (Author)

49

This well-worn F-4A-1 (75) was assigned to the 9th Photographic Reconnaissance Squadron (PRS) at Pandaveswar, India in early 1943. The F-4A-1 was based on the P-38E airframe, but had its nose-mounted guns replaced by camera equipment. The silver football-shaped housing atop the canopy enclosed an Automatic Direction Finding (ADF) antenna for long-range navigation assistance. This antenna was standard on F-4/F-5 Photo Lightnings assigned to the China-Burma-India (CBI) Theatre of Operations. The F-4A-1 is painted in the Haze Scheme of Flight Blue (FS35190) over Sky Base Blue (FS15123). (Vaclav Simecek)

An 8th PRS pilot enters his F-4A-1 at Guadalcanal's Fighter 2 airstrip in 1943. Although the insignia painted on the nose was previously believed to be from the 17th PRS, it is now believed to be for the 8th PRS. The individual aircraft number 67 appears in tape ahead of this badge. The F-4A-1 carried up to five Fairchild Camera and Instrument K-17 trimetregon (vertical and oblique) cameras for photographing enemy installations. The long nose gear door and side-opening canopy were both carried over from the P-38E. (Author's Collection)

Two K-17 fixed vertical cameras are mounted in the camera bay of this F-4-1-LO, modified from a standard P-38E. Each camera had a focal length of 6 inches (15.2 CM) and had a top-mounted film magazine for taking 250 exposures. The K-17s replaced the guns and ammunition, while small plates were riveted over the gun openings. Lockheed built the first of 94 F-4-1-LOs in December of 1941 and the type entered service with the 8th PRS at Townsville, Australia in the early spring of 1942. (Lockheed)

VIOLA was an F-5A-10-LO (299) assigned to the 8th PRS at Fighter 2 airstrip on Guadalcanal in 1943. It is painted in Haze Paint, an early attempt to camouflage reconnaissance aircraft in the air using various shades of blue. This aircraft – a conversion of the P-38G-10-LO – is equipped with Lockheed-designed 165 gallon (624.6 L) underwing fuel tanks. (Vaclav Simecek)

Reconnaissance Lightning cockpits were virtually identical to those of standard P-38 fighters; this F-5A cockpit is similar to that of the P-38G. The primary difference is the camera controls mounted on the central pedestal. F-4s and F-5s also lacked the gun sight, since their weapons were removed. Cockpit interiors were primarily Interior Green (FS34151) and Instrument Black (FS27038). (Lockheed)

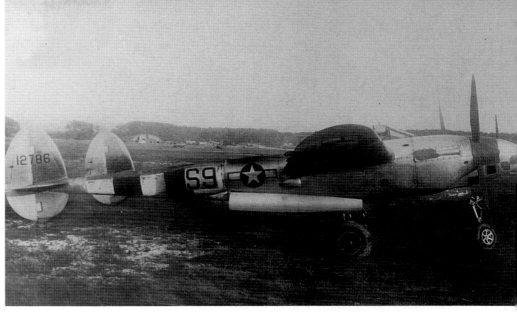

This F-5A-10-LO (S9/42-12786) was assigned to the 34th PRS, 10th Photographic Group in France during the 1944 Allied campaign. Its original Olive Drab over Neutral Gray camouflage was stripped to a natural metal finish. Two dice painted on the nose indicated the 'dicing' (highly dangerous) reconnaissance missions this and other F-5s flew prior to the D-Day landings on 6 June 1944. (Tom Ivie)

The F-5A/B Photo Lightning's camera bay was equipped for both oblique and vertical cameras. Two K-17s with 6 inch focal length lenses shot obliquely to port and starboard. Immediately behind were two additional K-17s fitted with 24 inch (61 CM) focal length lenses for vertical photography. Camera bays were painted Flat Black (FS37038) to eliminate lens glare from photographs. (Lockheed)

51

An F-5B-1-LO (42-67332) makes a test flight from Lockheed's Burbank, California plant in mid to late 1943. This Lightning variant combined the P-38J airframe with the same camera suite used on the earlier F-5A-10-LO derivative of the P-38G-10-LO. The aircraft is painted overall PRU Blue (FS35164), a British reconnaissance aircraft color also used on some UK-based USAAF F-5s. On 29 June 1943, the US national insignia was modified to include white side bars and flat Insignia Red (FS31136) trim. This trim was replaced by flat Insignia Blue (FS35044) from 17 September 1943. The Lockheed production batch number (43) is painted on the oblique camera window cover. The F-5B was the first reconnaissance variant equipped with a Sperry autopilot for long-range flights. (Lockheed)

Two F-4As – including 41-2239 – are parked at Longview airfield on Adak in the Aleutian Islands during the summer of 1942. These Photo Lightnings flew reconnaissance missions over Japanese targets on the nearby islands of Attu and Kiska, which Japan seized in early June of 1942. Steel Marston matting covered the muddy earth to form runways, taxiways, and dispersal points. Various tools, equipment, and tarpaulins were placed off the port side of the near F-4A, while another bundled tarpaulin covers the aft cockpit canopy section. An unknown unit insignia is painted on the radiator housing of the far F-4A, which also has a diagonal Orange Yellow stripe on the vertical tail. A Curtiss P-40 Warhawk undergoes maintenance in the background. (Lockheed)

A ground crewman carries a camera to PICTURE PACKING MAMA, an F-5E assigned to the 3rd Photographic Group in Italy in early 1945. This Group consisted of the 5th, 12th, and 23rd PRSs. Lockheed converted all 100 F-5Es from P-38J-10-LO airframes. Total Allied air superiority late in World War Two resulted in new F-5Es being delivered in natural metal, with Flat Black anti glare panels. (Author's Collection)

Three personnel from the 6th Photographic Reconnaissance Group (PRG) gather before one of their F-5Es (956) at Pitae Airfield on Morotai Island, Netherlands East Indies in 1945. This Group was formed with the 8th, 25th, and 26th PRSs. Bulged side windows for larger Fairchild K-22 oblique cameras distinguished the F-5E from earlier Photo Lightning variants. Eleven mission tally marks are painted in yellow on the aircraft's nose. (Author's Collection)

Ground crews service the starboard Allison V-1710 engine of a 25th PRS F-5B-1-LO (42-67354) at San Jose Air Base on Mindoro, the Philippines in late 1944. Two mechanics stand on a metal frame work platform to access the upper engine section. Well-worn nose and wing leading edges testify to the high mission tempo by 25th PRS pilots during the Philippine campaign. F-4/F-5 aircraft moved the radio antenna mast from the lower nose to the upper nose, which allowed room for the cameras. (Lockheed)

A 34th PRS, 10th PRG F-5B (S9/42-67112) flies over northern France during the fall of 1944. This Squadron deployed from England to France to support the Allied forces. The black and white D-Day invasion stripes were overpainted everywhere except the tail boom sides and undersurfaces by this date. Patchy PRU Blue paint was evidence of extensive maintenance performed at front-line airfields. (Tom Ivie)

A 34th PRS pilot stands in front of his F-5B (561) at Chateaudun, France in the late summer of 1944. Unusually, this aircraft mated an early F-4A nose onto a P-38J airframe. There was no provision for oblique cameras on this F-5B. Oval patches were riveted over the gun ports. The aircraft is equipped with 165 gallon drop tanks under the wings. (Author's Collection)

Gin was an F-5E-2-LO (721) serving with the 3rd PRG at Florence, Italy in late 1944. Lockheed's Dallas, Texas modification center converted 100 P-38J-15-LOs to F-5E-2-LO standard. This natural metal Lightning has red and white propeller spinners, while the vertical tail is black with an Orange Yellow number. (USAFM)

Pin-up art decorates the nose of "UNFAITHFUL," an F-5E-2-LO (43-28304) assigned to the 34th PRS, 10th PRG at Rennes, France in the summer of 1944. A K-17 camera was mounted behind the side bulge window for taking oblique photographs of the target area. White swastikas on the nose recorded missions flown against German targets. (Tom Ivie)

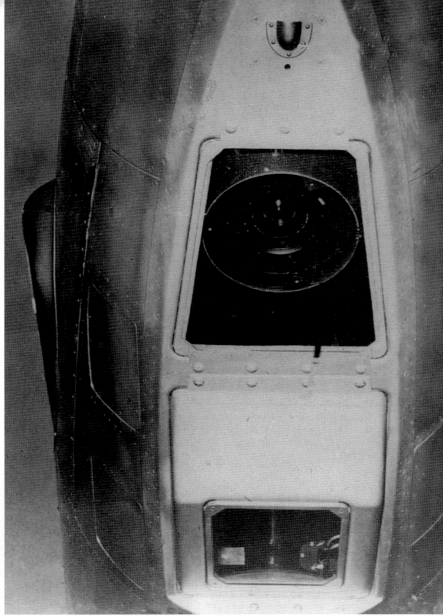

The F-5E's two vertical K-17 cameras took photographs through windows mounted on the nose undersurface. A 200 foot (61 M) long film strip was fed into each camera to record images. After returning to base, the film was downloaded and developed into standard 9 inch (22.9 CM) by 9 inch prints. A camera bay air cooling scoop is mounted ahead of the forward camera window, while the starboard oblique camera window protruded from the side. (Via Tom Ivie)

(Above Left) Access panels have been removed from the gun bay of 'Glacier Girl,' a P-38F-1-LO (41-7630) lost in the Greenland ice after a forced landing on 15 July 1942. The Lightning was recovered in 1992 and taken to Middlesboro, Kentucky for restoration to flying condition, which was completed in 2002. Belts of .50 caliber (12.7MM) ammunition are fed from their ammunition bins to the Browning M2 machine guns. Each bin held 500 rounds of ammunition, which was available in several types. These types included Armor Piercing (AP), Ball, Tracer, Incendiary, Armor Piercing Incendiary (API), and Armor Piercing Incendiary/Tracer (API/T). The air-cooled M2 machine gun had a muzzle velocity of 2900 feet (883.9 M) per second, a cyclic firing rate of 800 rounds per minute (RPM), and a range of 7400 yards (6766.6 M). Immediately aft of the machine guns is the 150 round ammunition drum for the 20MM Bendix M1 cannon. This weapon had a muzzle velocity of 2850 feet (868.7 M) per second and a cycling firing rate of 650 RPM. (John Clements)

(Above) Markings indicating 17 kills over Japanese aircraft are painted on the nose of Capt Tommy McGuire's P-38J PUDGY III (131, serial unknown) in May of 1944. He was commander of the 431st FS, 475th FG at Hollandia, New Guinea. A red devil is painted on the nose tip, with the gun camera aperture in the middle of its mouth. McGuire named all five of his P-38s PUDGY. (T.S. Shreve via David Menard)

(Left) The port gun bay door is slightly opened on The Fighter Collection's P-38J, restored in the markings of California Cutie (42-67916). Each door was hinged at the top to open upward and was locked in place using 12 Dzus quick-turn fasteners. This Lightning has 62 gallon (234.7 L) tanks fitted in the wing leading edges, which is indicated by the white cross on the lower nose. (Keith Melville)

A formation light panel was mounted on the fuselage nacelle undersurface, immediately aft of the nose landing gear bay. The three lights were (from front) red, blue, and yellow and were used during night operations. Some P-38s replaced the blue lamp with one of green. (Author)

A metal-covered aileron was mounted on the trailing edge of both port and starboard wings. This surface moved up or down to bank the aircraft according to input from the control column. The pitot tube mounted under the P-38J's port wing collected air speed data for cockpit instruments, including the air speed indicator. This tube was mounted under the nose on early Lightnings, but moved to the wing on the P-38F. (Detail & Scale Photo by Bert Kinzey)

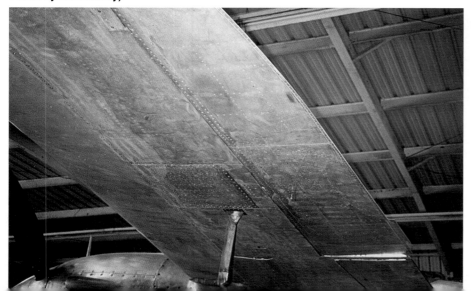

A small bluish green navigation light is mounted on the starboard outer wing panel undersurface. This lamp is repeated on the upper surface in the same area. Red lights were fitted to the same positions on the port wing. The pilot turned on the navigation lights from inside the cockpit for night flying. The P-38's wing had a dihedral (up angle from horizontal) of 5° 40 minutes. (Detail & Scale Photo by Bert Kinzey)

TURBO ANNY/MISSY LaRUE is an F-5E-3-LO (XX-G/44-28332) assigned to the 34th PRS, 69th Tactical Reconnaissance Group (TRG) at Haguenau, France in the spring of 1945. At least 120 mission markers are painted on the nose of this Lightning. A lens extension fit-ted under the forward vertical window accommodated a longer focal length camera. Trim on the nose tip, spinners, and upper and lower vertical tail tips is Orange Yellow. This same color with black trim is used for the lettering and numbering. (Chris Goodman via Art Krieger)

A 34th PRS F-5E (43-50304) is parked at Haguenau, France in early 1945. This aircraft also has the extended lens fairing under the nose. The F-5E was the primary reconnaissance aircraft of the US XIXth Tactical Air Corps, which supported the US Third Army's advance across France into Germany. This Lightning is painted Synthetic Haze Blue with Orange Yellow trim. (James V. Crow)

A chaff dispenser is mounted under the starboard wing of this 21st PRS F-5E (9008). This Squadron of the 5th PRG was based at Biak, New Guinea on 31 May 1945. This aircraft flew ahead of a force of B-29 Superfortress bombers and released chaff (aluminum strips) to jam Japanese radars. The F-5E then made a return pass and took bomb damage assessment photographs before heading home. (USAFM)

The F-5F-3-LO Darling Ruth Arlene (954) is parked at Clark AB, the Philippines while serving with the 17th PRS, 4th PRG in 1945-46. Several other F-5s assigned to this Squadron are parked in the background. The F-5F was based on the P-38L airframe, but incorporated a revised nose to house three vertical and two oblique cameras. The carriage of two 300 gallon (1135.6 L) drop tanks under the wings extended the Lightning's range to 1750 miles (2816.3 KM). This performance made the F-5 ideal for reconnaissance missions over the Japanese home islands late in World War Two. A dive flap is mounted under the port wing of this F-5F. (Art Krieger)

An F-5F-3-LO (44-24268) is parked outside the Dallas modification center after its conversion from a P-38L-4-LO. This variant was equipped with five K-17 cameras: two oblique mounted and three vertically mounted. The nose undersurface was deepened to accommodate the longer focal length vertical cameras. Most F-5Fs were assigned to USAAF units operating in the South Pacific. (USAFM)

The F-5F-3's port oblique camera window is smaller than the starboard window, although it had no adverse affect on camera performance. The enlarged nose undersurface had space for longer K-17 vertical cameras. There was an option for another camera directly in the nose for forward views. A loop shaped Automatic Direction Finding (ADF) antenna is mounted aft of the nose gear bay. (USAFM)

A 27th FS, 1st FG P-38J-15-LO (5/43-28650) returns to Lesina, Italy after a long-range escort mission in early 1945. Stabilizing wires for the 300 gallon drop tanks hang from the inner wing undersurfaces. Lightning pilots released the tanks when German fighters were encountered. The propeller spinners, wingtips, and aft tail booms were red on 27th FS P-38s. (USAF)

A 343rd FG P-38L-5-LO (44-26758) sits on the ramp at Adak, Aleutian Islands in 1945. The tail of another Lightning appears behind the near aircraft. The 343rd FG's P-38s were the first to engage the Japanese on 4 August 1942, when two P-38s downed a pair of Japanese seaplanes near Atka. The Group remained the first line of defense in North America's northern reaches until the war ended in 1945. (R. Arnold via David Menard)

Maj John Stafford fires the guns of a P-38J-15-LO (43-28859) over the Gulf of Mexico in 1944. Gas from the 20MM M1 cannon puffs back while the Lightning flies at low altitude. Olive Drab (FS34087) anti-glare panels are painted on the upper fuselage and inboard engine nacelles. There are no unit markings painted on this natural metal aircraft. The air exhaust flap on the engine nacelle and the aft radiator doors are in their normal closed position for flight. (Lockheed)

Lockheed Chief Test Pilot Milo Burcham flies YIPPEE, the 5000th P-38 built– a P-38J-20-LO (44-23296) – over Southern California on 17 May 1944. The Lightning was painted over-all red (approximately FS11310), with YIPPEE in white on the nose. This name was repeated in larger black-edged white letters under the wings. Considerable exhaust staining covered parts of the aft tail booms. Burcham flew YIPPEE over Lockheed's Burbank plant and other company facilities in the area. The aircraft was later stripped of its paint job and placed in USAAF service. (Lockheed)

The first F-5G conversion (44-25067) is parked at the Dallas Modification Center after its roll out in 1945. It lacks the ADF antenna later mounted under the nose. The last four digits of the serial number are painted on the nose, ahead of the oblique camera window. F-5Gs were equipped with two oblique and two vertical K-17 cameras, plus an additional forward-looking camera in the nose. (Lockheed)

NOSEY BUB was an F-5G assigned to the 41st PRS on Guam in mid-1945. The individual aircraft number 2 is painted on the aft radiator housing. This Lightning flew long-range photo reconnaissance missions over the Japanese home islands, which required using the ADF antenna mounted under the nose for navigation assistance. (James V. Crow)

LUSCIOUS ! LUCILLE was an F-5G-6-LO (44-26421) assigned to the 41st PRS at Northwest Field, Guam in 1945. This Lightning is equipped with a football-shaped Automatic Direction Finder (ADF) antenna under the nose. An ADF antenna homed in on radio signals sent by ground stations, which aided the pilot in long-range navigation. The F-5G mounted a forward-looking camera in the nose. Lockheed's Dallas modification center converted 63 P-38L-5-LOs into F-5G reconnaissance aircraft. (James V. Crow)

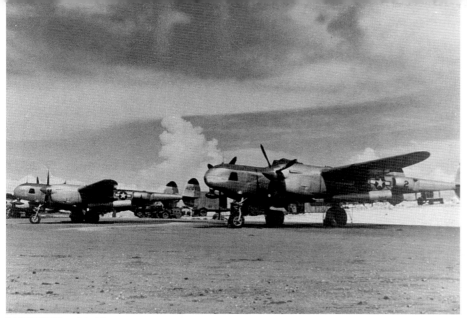

LUSCIOUS ! LUCILLE (44-26421) leads a ramp full of 41st PRS F-5Gs on Guam's Northwest Field in 1945. This Squadron was assigned to 20th Air Force, whose B-29 Superfortress bombers attacked the Japanese home islands from bases in the Marianas. Spinners, wingtips, and tail tips of the F-5Gs are painted red. (James V. Crow)

The Norden bombsight was mounted in the port side of the P-38J 'Droop Snoot' nose compartment. An optically flat panel in the bubble allowed for distortion-free sighting of the target. The bombardier entered his cramped station through a hatch in the floor. 'Droop Snoot' P-38Js carried up to 4000 pounds (1814.4 KG) of bombs under the wings. (Lockheed)

Lockheed converted 23 P-38Js to 'Droop Snoot' configuration in the early spring of 1944. All armament was removed and a Plexiglas bubble was installed in the nose. A bombardier sat in the nose, which was equipped with a Norden bombsight. Lockheed later made 100 'Droop Snoot' conversion kits for field modification of existing Lightnings. (Lockheed)

Lady Lou was a P-38J 'Droop Snoot' assigned to the 82nd FG at Vincenzo Airfield, Italy in early 1945. This aircraft lacks the narrow Plexiglas window just aft of the nose bubble, but retains the larger window further back. 'Droop Snoots' led fighter aircraft formations on high altitude horizontal bombing attacks. All aircraft in the formation dropped their bombs on the 'Droop Snoot' bombardier's command *"Bombs away!"* (USAFM)

A P-38L-5-LO (44-27112) sits alongside a second Lightning on the ramp at Chanute Army Air Base (AAB), Illinois in 1946. It is plainly marked apart from national insignia, serial number on the tail, and the aircraft-in-group number (37) on the radiator housing. The port radiator door is closed while on the ground. By 1946, the War Department's desire for an all-jet Air Force resulted in the P-38's rapid phase out from US service. (Col O.C. Griffith via David Menard)

Civilian contractors purchased several P-38s and F-5s after World War Two. The Lightnings were used for public relations flights and to transport executives to and from meetings. The J.D. Reed Co., a division of Mobiloil, owned this former F-5G (NX25Y). Its paint scheme included Mobiloil's Pegasus insignia on the fuselage and nacelles. (Dick Starinchak)

Another F-5G to see postwar civilian use was "BATTY BETTY" II (N67864). Jack Hardwick flew this Lightning to a sixth place finish in the Sohio Trophy event of the 1948 National Air Races in Cleveland, Ohio. Hardwick was nicknamed 'The Madman Muntz of the Air' after Los Angeles entrepreneur Earl 'Madman' Muntz, who was known for his low-cost television sets and outrageous sales pitches. The F-5G's race number (34) is painted on the engine nacelle. (Charles Trask)

Bill Ross of Chicago, Illinois purchased this P-38L-5-LO (44-53095, N9005R) in the early 1970s. He restored this Lightning, which he named *Der Gabelschwanz Teufel*, German for the Forked-Tail Devil – the nickname Luftwaffe pilots bestowed upon the P-38. This aircraft was parked at DuPage County Airport near Chicago. The Lightning had previously served as a gate guard in Honduras until it was returned to the US in the early 1960s. In 1987, Ross sold this P-38 to the Lone Star Flight Museum in Galveston, Texas. The museum has since repainted the Lightning as Charles MacDonald's fifth PUTT PUTT MARU. (David McLaren)

Two 1000 pound (453.6 KG) bombs are mounted under the wings of this P-38J at Lockheed's Burbank factory. Factory specifications called for a maximum ordnance load of 1600 pounds (725.8 KG) on each underwing pylon; however, this was often exceeded in service use. Underwing ordnance varied by both type and mission. (Lockheed)

Technicians of the 82nd FG added four additional inner wing pylons to this P-38J. Four 500 pound bombs are mounted on these added pylons, while two 165 gallon (624.6 L) drop tanks lie on the ground. These tanks were mounted on the standard pylons, between the bombs. Under this arrangement, the tanks had to be jettisoned first to allow the bombs to fall cleanly from the P-38. (Lockheed)

This 82nd FG P-38 was field-modified with an outer wing pylon to both port and starboard. Two 500 pound (226.8 KG) bombs are loaded onto this pylon, which could instead carry three 250 pound (113.4 KG) bombs or a drop tank. This freed the standard inner wing pylons for either drop tanks or additional ordnance. The 82nd FG flew from Vincenzo Airfield in Italy in 1944-45. (Lockheed)

Ground crew load a 1000 pound depth charge under the wing of the P-38J Irish Lassie. This Lightning was assigned to the 459th FS, 80th FG at Chittagong, India (now in Bangladesh) in late 1944. Aircraft and surface ships dropped depth charges on submerged submarines. This was a rare weapon for the Lightning, which seldom flew anti-submarine patrols. (USAFM)

Both early and late P-38 variants were capable of carrying three-tube bazooka rocket launchers on either nose side. This set is mounted on the port side fuselage of a P-38G assigned to the 80th FG. The highly effective bazooka tubes fired a 5 inch (12.7 CM) rocket. Lightnings of the 80th FG fired bazookas against Japanese rail and road traffic in neighboring Burma and Thailand. (Lockheed)

Lockheed equipped this P-38L with 14 underwing 'zero-launch stubs' – seven per wing. Each stub mounted a 5 inch High Velocity Air Rocket (HVAR). This offered greater firepower than the three-tube bazooka launchers; however, Lockheed and the USAAF standardized on the five-rocket 'tree' launcher for P-38J/L/M aircraft. (Lockheed)

A P-38L equipped with two five-round underwing 'tree' rocket launchers taxis out for a test flight. This was one of several rocket-firing arrangements Lockheed developed for this Lightning variant. Each 5 inch HVAR was 72 inches (182.9 CM) long, weighed 140 pounds (63.5 KG), and had an effective range of 400 yards (365.8 M). (Lockheed)

No rockets are loaded onto the port underwing 'tree' launcher on this P-38L. The launcher consisted of fore-and-aft pylons, which captured lugs mounted on each rocket. The HVARs were fired electrically in port and starboard pairs to avoid asymmetrical loads on the fighter. The 'tree' launcher was standard on late P-38s, but these rockets were seldom used in combat. (Lockheed)

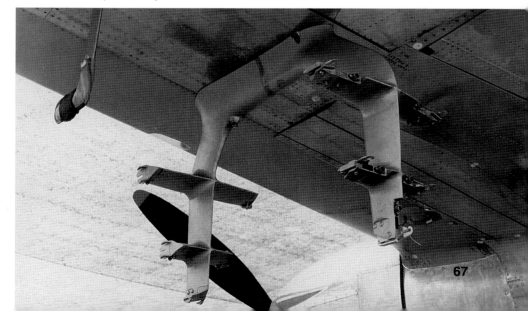

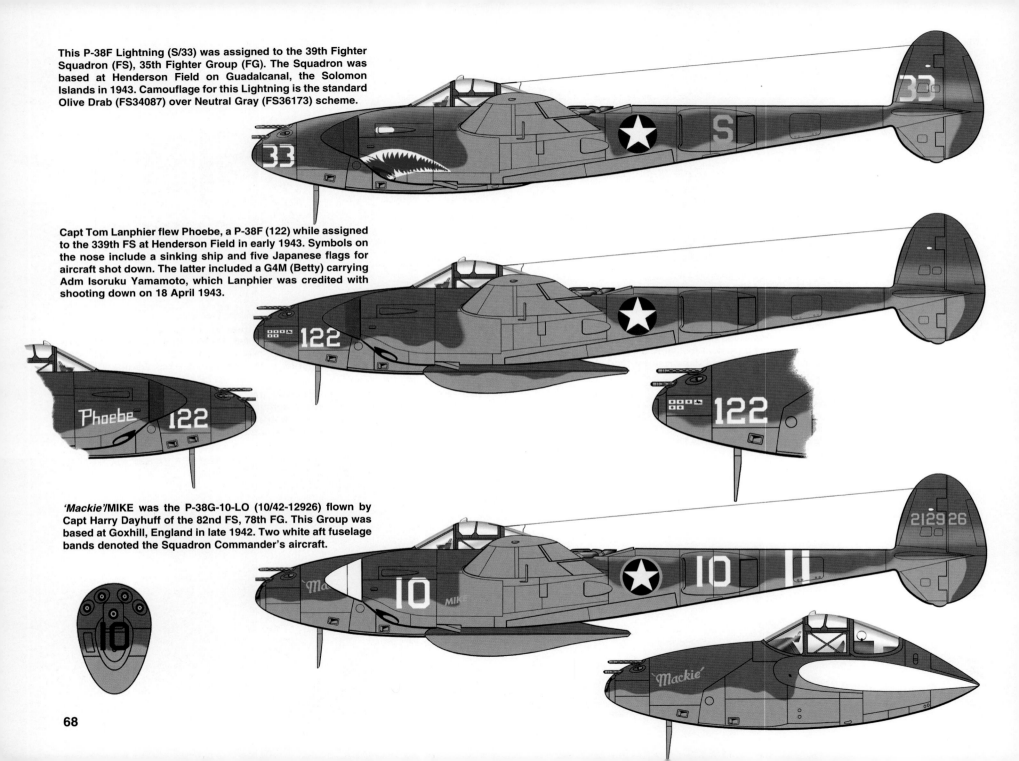

This P-38F Lightning (S/33) was assigned to the 39th Fighter Squadron (FS), 35th Fighter Group (FG). The Squadron was based at Henderson Field on Guadalcanal, the Solomon Islands in 1943. Camouflage for this Lightning is the standard Olive Drab (FS34087) over Neutral Gray (FS36173) scheme.

Capt Tom Lanphier flew Phoebe, a P-38F (122) while assigned to the 339th FS at Henderson Field in early 1943. Symbols on the nose include a sinking ship and five Japanese flags for aircraft shot down. The latter included a G4M (Betty) carrying Adm Isoruku Yamamoto, which Lanphier was credited with shooting down on 18 April 1943.

'Mackie'/MIKE was the P-38G-10-LO (10/42-12926) flown by Capt Harry Dayhuff of the 82nd FS, 78th FG. This Group was based at Goxhill, England in late 1942. Two white aft fuselage bands denoted the Squadron Commander's aircraft.

1/Lt P.V. Morriss flew *Hold Everything*, a P-38G (117) with the 431st FS, 475th FG. The Group was based at Dobodura, New Guinea in late 1943. His two victories to date were recorded on the fuselage. Morriss had five total 'kills' by mid-1944.

This P-38H-1-LO (66/42-66685) was named *Hot Pants* and assigned to the 339th FS, 347th FG on Guadalcanal in late 1943. The Lockheed construction number 1196 painted on the nose was retained when the Lightning entered USAAF service.

The F-4-1-LO FOTO-JO (A-45) was an F-4-1-LO converted to an F-4C. This Lightning was assigned to the 8th Photographic Reconnaissance Group (PRG) at Barrackpur, near Karachi, India (now in Pakistan). Two .50 caliber (12.7ᴍᴍ) machine guns were retained in the nose of this F-4, which is camouflaged in Medium Green (FS34092) over Light Blue (FS15102).

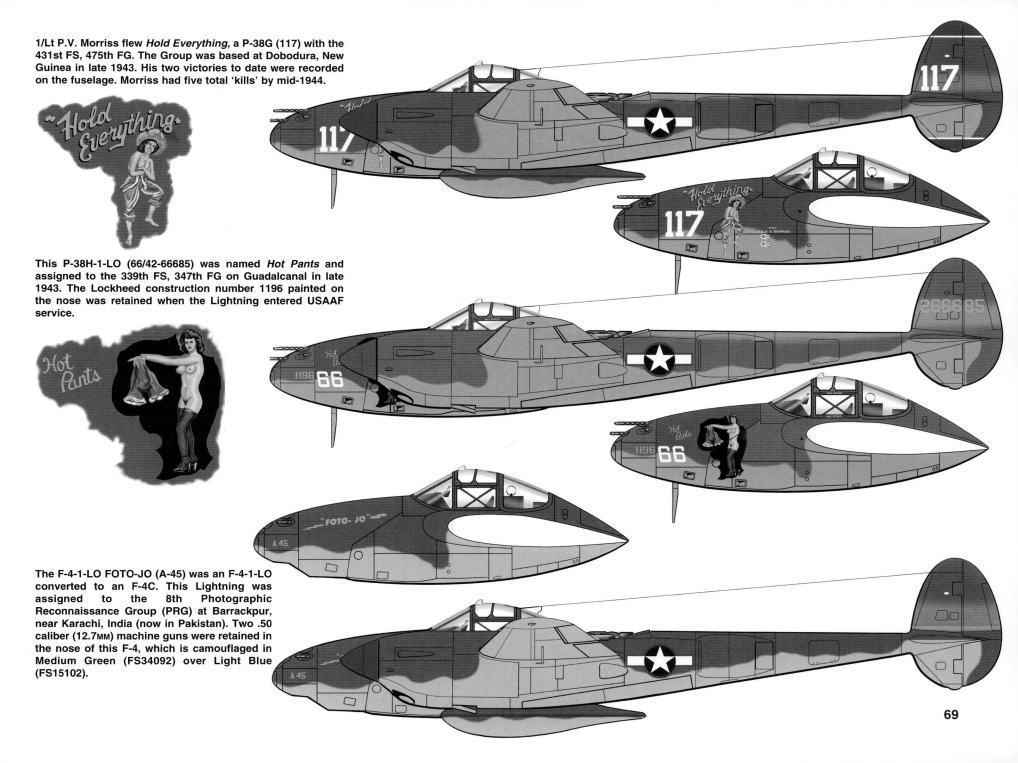

69

(Above) The first P-38M Night Lightning (44-26865) is displayed after rollout from Lockheed's Dallas modification center in July of 1945. The P-38M was a standard P-38L modified with a Western Electric AN/APS-4 X-band airborne intercept radar housed in a small pod under the nose. The VHF radio mast was relocated from the nose to the port tail boom. The aft fuselage was modified to carry a radar operator immediately aft of the pilot. Lockheed converted 75 P-38Ls into P-38Ms in mid-1945. (Lockheed)

(Left) A P-38M (44-27234) making a stateside test flight is painted overall glossy Jet Black (FS17038), the standard USAAF night fighter color scheme. The serial and nose numbers are Insignia Red (FS11136). Panels surrounding the supercharger exhausts were left in natural metal, along with the oval landing gear check mirrors on the inboard engine nacelles. Five-round rocket 'trees' are mounted under the wings, although the P-38M was designed for the night intercept role. (Lockheed)

Aft-hinged bubble canopies covered the cockpits for the pilot and the Radar Operator (RO), who sat aft and slightly above the pilot. The RO's armored seat was bolted to a reconfigured aft cockpit extension and his legs sat flat on the floor. The radar scope eye shield protrudes from the scope, while radar controls are mounted below this instrument. (USAFM)

The RO was forced to sit in a hunched over position once his canopy was closed. He had to retain this position for much of the mission. The pilot's enclosure included an upper canopy with rear view mirror and two roll-up side windows. Two fuel filler caps are marked in red near the cockpit. (USAFM)

The P-38M's pod-mounted AN/APS-4 was an Active Seeker Homing (ASH) radar also used on the US Navy and Marine Corps' Grumman F6F-3N/5N Hellcat night fighters. Conical flash suppressors on the guns' muzzles reduced the glare from gunfire at night, which would cause the pilot to lose his night vision. Covers were placed over the two starboard .50 caliber cartridge ejection chutes. Glossy Insignia Red numbers and stenciling were painted over the overall glossy Jet Black scheme. (Lockheed)

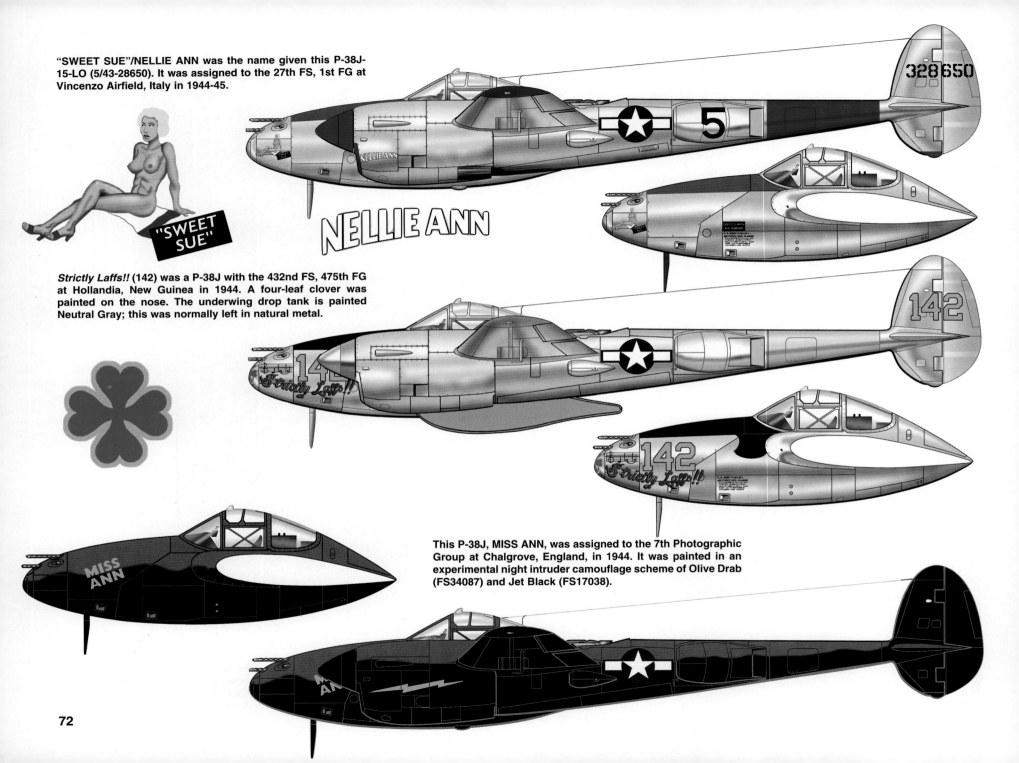

"SWEET SUE"/NELLIE ANN was the name given this P-38J-15-LO (5/43-28650). It was assigned to the 27th FS, 1st FG at Vincenzo Airfield, Italy in 1944-45.

Strictly Laffs!! (142) was a P-38J with the 432nd FS, 475th FG at Hollandia, New Guinea in 1944. A four-leaf clover was painted on the nose. The underwing drop tank is painted Neutral Gray; this was normally left in natural metal.

This P-38J, MISS ANN, was assigned to the 7th Photographic Group at Chalgrove, England, in 1944. It was painted in an experimental night intruder camouflage scheme of Olive Drab (FS34087) and Jet Black (FS17038).

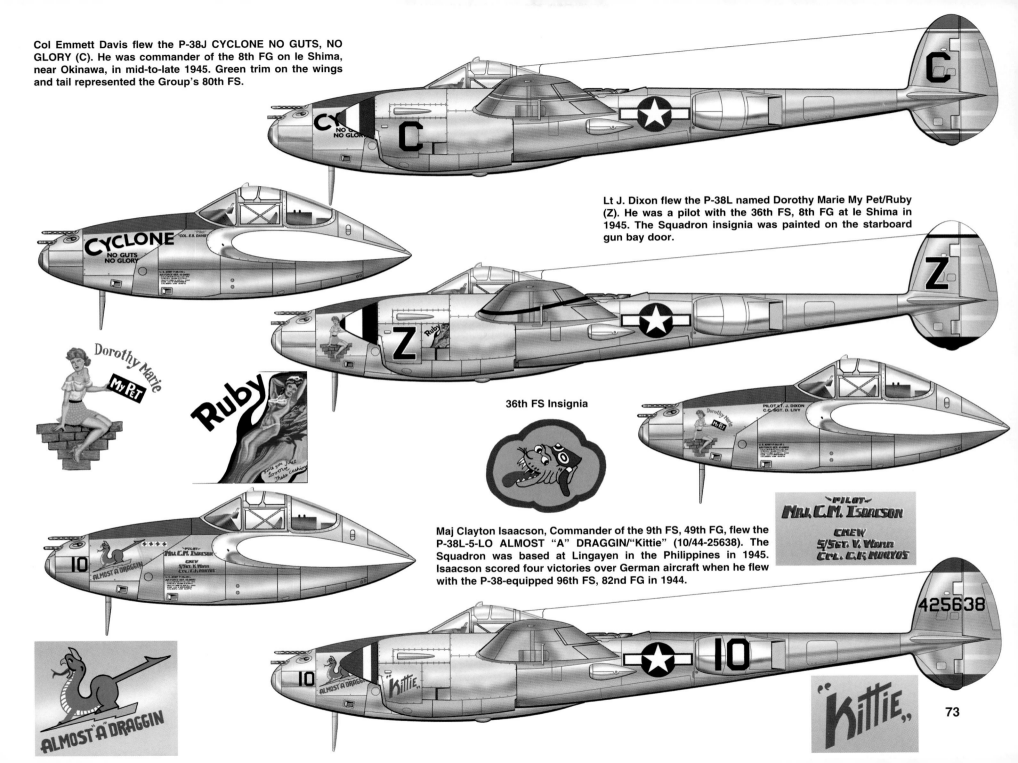

Col Emmett Davis flew the P-38J CYCLONE NO GUTS, NO GLORY (C). He was commander of the 8th FG on Ie Shima, near Okinawa, in mid-to-late 1945. Green trim on the wings and tail represented the Group's 80th FS.

Lt J. Dixon flew the P-38L named Dorothy Marie My Pet/Ruby (Z). He was a pilot with the 36th FS, 8th FG at Ie Shima in 1945. The Squadron insignia was painted on the starboard gun bay door.

36th FS Insignia

Maj Clayton Isaacson, Commander of the 9th FS, 49th FG, flew the P-38L-5-LO ALMOST "A" DRAGGIN/"Kittie" (10/44-25638). The Squadron was based at Lingayen in the Philippines in 1945. Isaacson scored four victories over German aircraft when he flew with the P-38-equipped 96th FS, 82nd FG in 1944.

73

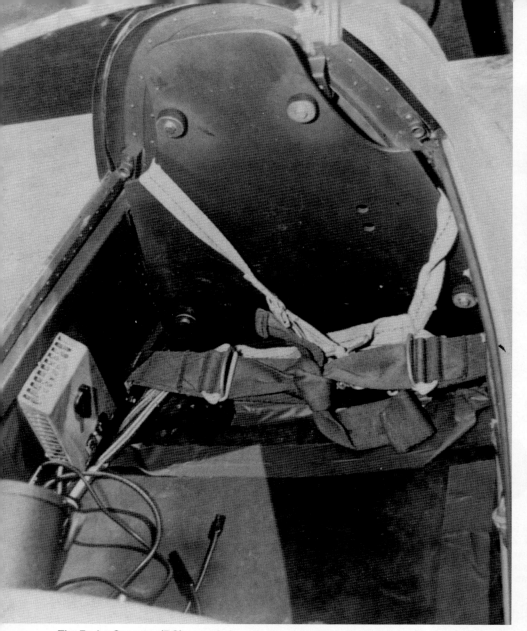

An electrical circuit box is mounted on the port wall of the RO's cockpit. Cables running from this box supplied power to the P-38M's electrical systems, including the radar, radio, interior and exterior lights, and dive flaps. The viewing hood was removed from the AN/APS-4 radar scope atop the instrument panel. The RO's oxygen hose lies on the cockpit floor beside the oxygen regulator. (USAFM)

Intercom and radio controls are mounted along the starboard RO's cockpit wall. Cables draped over the cockpit floor plugged into his helmet for both transmission and receiving. Radar controls are located immediately below the radar scope. The generator servicing the AN/APR-4 and its associated equipment was located on the lower port front section of the cockpit. The RO's cockpit shared few controls with those of the pilot. (USAFM)

The Radar Operator (RO) occupied an austere position in the P-38M's aft cockpit. This station was little more than an armored seat back atop a flat piece of plywood floor. The plywood was located over the old radio equipment bay on the P-38L. Shoulder and lap belts secured the RO to his seat, while his shoulders were stooped to clear the canopy and his legs were laid out flat on the floor. This arrangement resulted in a most uncomfortable ride for the RO. (USAFM)

T-shaped airborne intercept radar antennas were mounted on the P-38M's outboard wing panels, immediately forward of the flaps. This antenna was first tested on a natural metal P-38L-5-LO (44-25237) used to evaluate the P-38M's systems. Signals from this antenna alerted the RO to enemy aircraft below him. (USAFM)

Additional T-shaped antennas were fitted to the horizontal stabilizer extensions, which allowed for aft quarter radar coverage. The stabilizer extensions were fixed surfaces that added a measure of stability to the Lightning. The black radio call numbers painted on the vertical tail (425237) had the last number of the fiscal year (44) preceding the rest of the serial number. (USAFM)

1/Lt Johnny Brewer (right) and 1/Lt David Hopwood stand before their P-38M "SHADY LADY" (44-27245). This Night Lightning was among a handful of aircraft operational with the 418th Night Fighter Squadron (NFS) at Atsugi, Japan in late 1945. The 75 P-38Ms built from P-38Ls arrived too late to see action before World War Two ended on 14 August 1945. Subsequently, they were deployed with the US occupation forces in Japan. The Jet Black overall finish displayed signs of wear. (David Hopwood via Warren Thompson)

This F-5A-LO, STINKY 2 (301/40), was assigned to the 9th Photo Reconnaissance Squadron (PRS), 8th Photo Reconnaissance Group (PRG) at Karachi, India in the late summer of 1943. It is painted in a Haze scheme for USAAF photo reconnaissance aircraft. Upper surfaces were Sky Base Blue (FS15123), with Flight Blue (FS35190) sides and pale blue undersurfaces.

Lt L.Q. Mettes flew MISSOURI OUTLAW, an F-5G-6-LO (B5/42-68193) assigned to the 28th PRS, 9th PRG. The Squadron was based at Saipan in the Marianas in early 1945.

MISSOURI OUTLAW

Mission Marks on MISSOURI OUTLAW

28th PRS Insignia

This F-5E-LO (058/44-25058) was assigned to the 8th PRS, 6th PRG at Dulag AB, the Philippines in 1945. The Squadron insignia was painted on the radiator housing, while the Group emblem appeared on the vertical stabilizer.

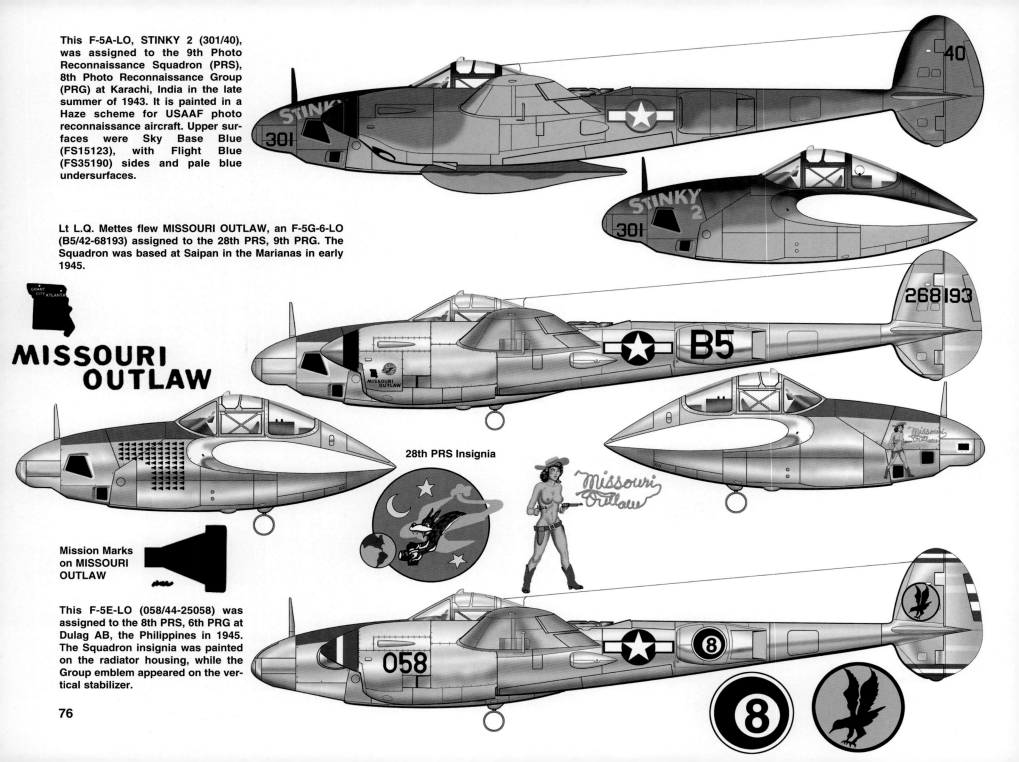

Capt Hershel Ezell, Jr. flew EZE DOES IT, a P-38J 'Droop Snoot.' The 77th FS, 20th FG operated this Lightning from Kings Cliffe, England in June of 1944. Four mission tally marks are painted on the nose after the name.

PEGGY ANN was an F-5G-6-LO (22/44-26438) assigned to the 41st PRS at Northwest Field, Guam in 1945. The Lightning is equipped with a football-shaped Automatic Direction Finder (ADF) antenna on the nose undersurface.

"SHADY LADY"/"SNOOKS" was the P-38M (44-27245) piloted by 1/Lt Johnny Brewer of the 418th NFS, with 1/Lt David Hopwood as the radar operator. This unit was part of the US occupation forces and was based at Atsugi, Japan in late 1945.

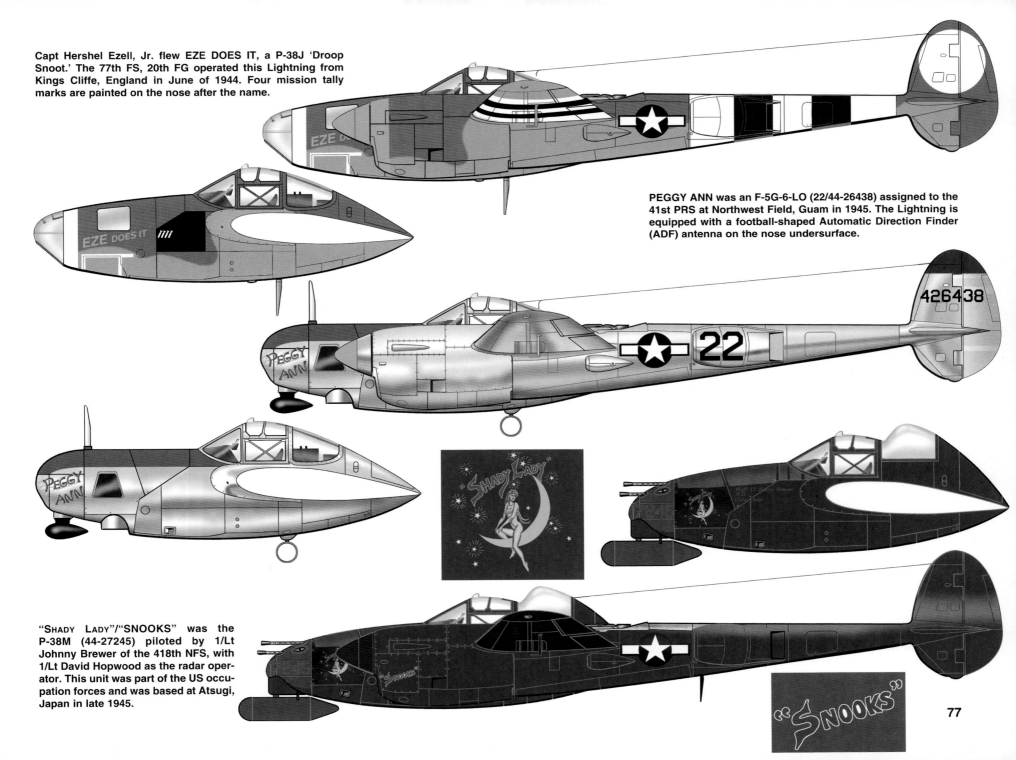

Maj James Watkins flew *Charlcie Jeanne*, a P-38J assigned to the 9th FS, 49th FG at Lingayen, the Philippines in early 1945. Japanese flags indicating Watkins' 12 victories are painted on the nose. His first ten 'kills' came while flying P-38s for the 9th FS in mid-1943. The outer port .50 caliber machine gun was removed from this Lightning and its opening faired over. (Col J. Watkins)

This P-38L-5-LO (100/44-25471) was the last of Col Charles MacDonald's five Lightnings named PUTT PUTT MARU. He flew this aircraft while commanding the 475th FG at Lingayen in the spring of 1945. MacDonald shot down 27 Japanese aircraft, which made him the fifth-leading USAAF ace of the conflict. (Don Garrett)

Maj Tommy McGuire poses before PUDGY (V), the last of the P-38s he flew for the 431st FS, 475th FG. Thirty victory marks are painted on the aircraft's nose in December of 1944. He became the second highest scoring US ace of World War Two with 38 victories. McGuire was killed during a mission over Negros Island, the Philippines on 7 January 1945. (Don Garrett)

(Above) A ground crewman stands before ALMOST "A" DRAG-GIN/"Kittie," the P-38L-5-LO (10/44-25638) flown by Maj Clayton Isaacson. He was assigned to the 9th FS, 49th FG at Lingayen Airfield in 1945. Four black swastikas on white rectangles denoted German aircraft Isaacson shot down while flying Lightnings for the 96th FS in the Mediterranean Theater in 1944. The .50 caliber machine guns were removed from this P-38L's nose. (Lockheed)

(Above Right) Capt Robert DeHaven stands before his P-38L (13), which is parked on the steel matted ramp at Lingayen in late 1944. Japanese 'Rising Sun' flags painted on the nose record his 14 total victories. DeHaven was assigned to the 7th FS, 49th FG, for which he flew P-40s on his first nine 'kills' before transitioning to the Lightning. (Lockheed)

(Right) Maj Dick Bong, America's all-time 'Ace of Aces,' poses before a P-38L painted in the markings of his last combat aircraft, MARGE. A photograph of his fiancée (later wife) Marge Vattendahl is glued to the port gun bay door. Bong scored 40 victories over Japanese aircraft in various P-38s between 27 December 1942 and 17 December 1944. He shot down his first 21 aircraft while flying with the 9th FS, 49th FG, while the final 19 came on assignment with the Fifth Fighter Command. On 12 December 1944, Bong was awarded the Medal of Honor for his actions during World War Two. He was killed test flying the Lockheed P-80 Shooting Star jet fighter at Burbank, California on 6 August 1945. (Lockheed)

More World War Two Aircraft
from squadron/signal publications

In Action Series

1030 Bf 110 Zerstörer

1059 A6M Zero

1106 P-61 Black Widow

1145 F4U Corsair

1181 Petlyakov Pe-2

Walk Around Series

5507 P-51D Mustang

5508 P-40 Warhawk

5509 F6F Hellcat

5513 Allison Eng. Mustangs

5516 B-17 Flying Fortress

For a complete listing of squadron/signal books, go to www.squadron.com